"What a gem!
We love the little
one.
Only here for the
weekend from
London ... but will
be back!

to

WE
BRUNCH
HARD!

from two
imperfect people
thank you for a
perfect evening.

Jonathan ; ?

That pork chop
changed my life.
Thank you.

Thanks for
heavy pour

of va"
See you oming again

Jason + Dani

Food was fabulous!
Thank you for finding
us a table!

This might be the
meal that gets
us back together

xo

Only Cool People
eat at the Bar

JUST ANOTHER
GREAT
NEW YORK
MOMENT!

Mihera Avi

AT DOUBLE
DIGIT VISITS
BETTER THAN
EVER!

♡ the BURGER!

Couldn't think
of a better
way to spend
a Tuesday evening

"I was born on Oct.
30th, 1945. When Mom
was taking me home
from the French Hospi.
on 30th Street,
the nurse found a
lady bug on my
bathrobe. This is said
to be a sign of
good luck."

75 Recipes for
Satisfying, Shareable Comfort Food

BIG
LOVE
COOKING

JOEY CAMPANARO

with Theresa Gambacorta

Photography by Con Poulos

CHRONICLE BOOKS
SAN FRANCISCO

Library of Congress Cataloging-in-Publication Data:

Names: Campanaro, Joey, author. | Gambacorta, Theresa, author. |
   Poulos, Con, photographer.
Title: Big love cooking / Joey Campanaro with Theresa Gambacorta ;
   photography by Con Poulos.
Description: San Francisco : Chronicle Books, 2020. | Includes index. |
Identifiers: LCCN 2020004851 | ISBN 9781452178639 (hardcover) |
   ISBN 9781452178974 (ebook)
Subjects: LCSH: Cooking, Italian. | Cooking, American.
Classification: LCC TX723 .C28145 2020 | DDC 641.5945—dc23
   LC record available at https://lccn.loc.gov/2020004851

Manufactured in China.

FSC
www.fsc.org
MIX
Paper from
responsible sources
FSC™ C008047

Food styling by **PAUL GRIMES**.

Prop styling by **LITTLE OWL TEAM**.

Design by **LIZZIE VAUGHAN**.

Typeset by **HOWIE SEVERSON**.

Typeset in Mrs. Eaves, Mr. Eaves Modern, and Saveur Sans.

10 9 8 7 6 5 4 3 2 1

Chronicle books and gifts are available at special quantity discounts
to corporations, professional associations, literacy programs, and
other organizations. For details and discount information, please
contact our premiums department at corporatesales@chroniclebooks.com
or at 1-800-759-0190.

CHRONICLE BOOKS LLC
680 Second Street
San Francisco, California 94107
www.chroniclebooks.com

DEDICATION

For my mother, Patricia, and her mother, Rosie Bova—
my "mom-mom." And the loving, intelligent,
beautiful, and powerful women who have influenced
me in becoming the person I am today.

CONTENTS

FOREWORD

I had reason to believe that the restaurant gods were taunting me. Over the years, a small storefront half a block from my house, in Greenwich Village, was occupied by one restaurant after another, and none of them turned out to be where I wanted to eat.

My neighbors claim that only a few restaurants ever did business in that space; to me, it seemed like dozens. As each renovation began, I'd try to divine from the building permits pasted in the window which kind of restaurant would emerge. I had big dreams—a Chinese restaurant serving the food of a province so culinarily superior that when its inhabitants visit Szechuan or Hunan they always bring their own lunch, for instance, or a fried chicken joint whose cook had, miraculously, replicated the recipe of the legendary Kansas City panfryer Chicken Betty Lucas.

I don't remember the names of the establishments that appeared instead, dashing my dreams. I do remember that one of them served the sort of overcomplicated food that reminded me of the generic restaurant I used to refer to as La Maison de la Casa House, Continental Cuisine.

Then, in 2006, along came Joey Campanaro and Little Owl. I realized that this was what I'd been waiting for all along—a place with a neighborhood restaurant's feel and a destination restaurant's food, a place where a casually dressed waiter could be taking your order for "gravy meatball sliders" as well as for "Parmesan truffle asparagus." And it was so close that I began referring to one table as my UPS table, since it offered a view that enabled me to intercept anyone who was about to make a delivery to my house. I might have concluded that I was, at last, being rewarded for some childhood good deed, except that, offhand, I couldn't remember any childhood good deeds that might qualify.

After a dozen years, my craving for the aforementioned gravy meatball sliders still approaches an addiction. Others are similarly afflicted. Gravy meatball sliders are Little Owl's best-known dish, despite competition from the pork-chop-with-butter-beans faction. It's in keeping with the spirit of the place that its best-known dish is not something Joey Campanaro developed while working in some of the country's most distinguished restaurants but something his grandmother made for him when he was growing up in South Philly. The proprietors of La Maison de la Casa House, Continental Cuisine would not approve of putting it on the menu of a restaurant that serves lobster bisque and filet mignon. Chicken Betty Lucas would.

—Calvin Trillin

INTRODUCTION

My earliest childhood memory is waking up to the smell of garlic, onions, and oil from browning meatballs, wafting through our row house on the 500 block of Queen Street in Queen Village, Philadelphia, in preparation for the Sunday gravy—by the way, we call it *gravy*, not *sauce*; it's a South Philly thing. The huge pot of tomato-based gravy was filled with fennel-spiked sweet sausage, pork ribs, meat-balls, flank steak braciole, and if we were lucky, a gelatinous pig's foot that us kids could pick at in the kitchen. I can still see the windows fogging up from the steam as I'd watch my grandmother Rosie Bova or my mom, Patricia, guarding the pot, gently corralling the meats into place and tenderly dressing the meatballs inside as they lifted some of the dark, rich gravy over them by the spoonful. This feeling of waking up to the Sunday gravy ritual can only be described as *big love*.

You should know, however, that my South Philly upbringing wasn't always Sunday gravy–colored sunsets and delicious, gooey pig feet surprises. Admittedly, it was at times pretty rough. My mother worked full time while raising six kids—four of her own plus my two cousins. My father was a Philadelphia fireman in the 1970s who dealt with one of the inner city's most devastating blazes. By the time I was fifteen, they were separated. Oftentimes, I'd be sent over to my grandmother's house

and I'd help her make silky homemades—a South Philly catchall phrase for fresh pasta. I'd delight in draping the freshly cut strips of dough over a broomstick that she'd lay across two dining room chairs so they could dry. Her cooking embodied humility and authenticity. It was also borne of an Italian immigrant work ethic: adapt, get creative, and get your hands dirty. I call it *do what ya gotta do*. I'll never forget my mom hustling out a simple but deeply satisfying one-pan dish of chicken legs, escarole, and white beans to feed her brood after a long workday. And it is to her and my grandmother that I owe my passion for making delicious food and feeding people.

It was that combo of a *do what ya gotta do* mind-set and *big love* feeling that propelled me into a career as chef. Well, my career actually began with a teenager's desire to buy a boat so that I could fish down at the Jersey Shore, where my father had a house. The conversation went like this:

Me: Dad, I want a boat.

Dad: Then get a job.

So, I got a job as a dishwasher at a New Jersey seafood restaurant and was hooked by the camaraderie and energy of the business (and became an excellent fisherman).

I also knew that, more than anything, I wanted my boss's job!

While majoring in restaurant management in college, I spent a riveting semester in Italy, studying early Etruscan architecture and culture and exploring the *abbondanza* of the Italian countryside. A few years later, I traveled to France, where I studied winemaking and deepened my passion for the Mediterranean. It wasn't lost on me that the pure, uncomplicated flavors I'd learned to use while in Europe echoed the flavors I had grown up with. After college, I cooked my way through some of America's top restaurants in Philadelphia, Los Angeles, and New York, where I mastered skills taught to me from the brightest chef minds in the business, including Neil Murphy, Andrew Humbert, Joachim Splichal, Jimmy Bradley, and Jonathan Waxman.

In 2004, I took on the role of a lifetime as executive chef of Pace, a 130-seat Italian restaurant in Tribeca, where I oversaw a dizzying selection of regional Italian dishes that were an Italophile's dream. When Pace closed, I found myself in a funk. One day, my former wife, Paula, found a tiny space for rent on the corner of Bedford and Grove Streets in the West Village and demanded that I call the landlord. It was that fateful call that awakened my dream of being my own boss and creating a neighborhood spot where I could conjure up the big love of my Italian-American South Philly childhood and put it on people's plates.

Little Owl opened in the spring of 2006, and it almost immediately became synonymous with my meatball sliders. Of course, they're my grandmother Rosie Bova's recipe—a blend of beef, pork, and veal that I sit on homemade buns made from a simple pizza dough recipe spiked with pecorino cheese. At the time I wasn't even thinking about starting a trend. I just wanted to create meatballs that my guests could eat with their hands.

With a name like *Little Owl*, it often comes as a surprise to guests when they discover so many Italian-American favorites on my menu. But there are a couple of reasons for this decidedly un-Italian name for my restaurant. First, Little Owl's name was taken from a historical landmark home directly across the street from us on 17 Grove Street that has a gorgeous (big) ceramic owl on top of its Italianate cornice roof to scare away New York City pigeons (they still perch there). And the vibe in my tiny space is definitively quirky, with a spirit that echoes the bohemian history of Greenwich Village. And most important, in a culinary world where everyone else is the authority on "authentic" Italian food, I wanted to create some distance from my exclusively Italian-American identity. I find great irony in this truth of mine. In order to finally come home to myself, I had to disown a little bit of my heritage to thrive as a restaurateur. I like to think that

I hedged my bets on the under-promise/over-deliver approach in my business model! There is nothing about the name *Little Owl* that says, "The pasta is great there!" and so I relish the surprise of our guests when they discover a bowl of ethereal, homemade ricotta cavatelli in tomato bacon broth. Also, an unassuming name like *Little Owl* affords me wiggle room to play with Mediterranean flavors and American regional dishes in my culinary expertise. And so it was within this distancing that I found my identity: a South Philly old-school grand-mom style chef who loves to cook Italian-American comfort foods in the context of my Mediterranean zeal for freshness, seasonality, and bold flavors.

All these recipes dive into that well of childhood comfort and memory that I call *big love*. And their history lies at the intersection of Queen Village and the West Village. So you'll find Little Owl favorites alongside my family recipes. You'll discover where the humble, homemade meatball gave rise to New York City trendsetting inventiveness. Where the old-world sensibility that I was blessed to be born into merges with the preparedness and skillfulness of my culinary discipline. Like my childhood adoration of pork and beans, grown up and brought to life in my double-cut pork chop that I sit on a glorious mound of Parmesan cheese–spiked butter beans (the huge cut harkens back to the kind of chop you'd find at a red-checkered-tablecloth joint in my neighborhood where somebody's uncle sits on the edge of his seat, napkin tucked into his collar, ready to pounce). There is nothing fragile or careful about these recipes. They are not a peck on the cheek. They are a warm embrace. After a lifetime of cooking, I have come to know this to be true: Big love has a following. So let's get the gravy going.

BIG LOVE PANTRY

The delight of *Big Love Cooking* is to create delicious, transporting comfort food with fresh ingredients that are readily available at the supermarket. So there's no wild goose chase here. Growing up, my mom stored ingredients on a lazy Susan that spun around to reveal a treasure trove of olive oils, spices, and herbs that were essential to the magic she created in our South Philly row house. Being a New York City chef with a tiny restaurant space, and an even tinier apartment, storage is reserved for only the most necessary ingredients. Just a note on fresh items: In all of my recipes, I use large organic brown eggs, whole milk, and unsalted butter.

Flours

I use organic unbleached all-purpose Beehive flour and I recommend that you look for any hard, red winter wheat flours. These hard wheat flours are the most versatile and are excellent for making pizza dough, biscuits, and fresh pasta. The protein content is higher than a softer cake flour, resulting in a well-structured, toothsome pasta and pizza crust. Also, all-purpose flour is excellent for my recipes since I use fresh yeast as a leavening agent. Other recipes that call for a specific flour benefit from the use of a natural starter instead of yeast. The choice of some chefs to use semolina in their pasta recipes and *tipo* OO flour for pizza dough speaks more about cooking style than any hard-and-fast rule. For making homemade pasta and pizza, I also keep cornmeal around for dusting any surfaces the dough contacts to prevent it from sticking. For whipping up my Whole Wheat Pancakes with Berries (page 33), you'll want to have whole wheat flour on hand. Look for Bob's Red Mill or King Arthur flours. For a deliciously nutty topping for a variety of seasonal fruit crumble desserts, use almond flour.

Herbs and Spices

The herbs used in these recipes are fresh, with the exception of dried, wild Calabrian oregano. Fresh herbs are just better for my taste. My grandmother would use fresh oregano in the summer and dried in the winter, and you can do the same. Fresh oregano is great in Spaghetti and Clams (page 107), but I prefer to use dried in my grandmother's pizza dough.

Use these fresh herbs in big love cooking: garlic, fresh bay leaf, rosemary, thyme, chives, cilantro, tarragon, basil, mint, dill, fresh horseradish, and Italian flat-leaf parsley. They are all easy to find, but even easier to grow! I have an outdoor terrace set up with pots of herbs, peppers, and tomatoes in the spring and summer. But fresh herbs grow just as well indoors on a windowsill. And it feels good to snip off a little at a time, just when you need them.

Note: When using woody-stemmed herbs, like rosemary, thyme, or tarragon, you can simply de-stem them by pinching the stem near the top and running your fingers down the length of the stem. For soft herbs, such as parsley, basil, cilantro, and dill, remove the leaves from their stalks by gently picking them off and chopping, as called for in the recipe.

Additionally, you'll want to stock your cupboards with these dried spices and herbs: dried bay leaf, celery salt, red pepper flakes, chili powder, Madras curry powder, cumin, coriander, cayenne, paprika, Coleman's mustard powder, turmeric, fennel seeds, whole black peppercorns, whole white peppercorns, nutmeg, clove, ground cinnamon, and cinnamon sticks.

I use a spice mix that was developed years ago while I was the executive chef at Jimmy Bradley's restaurant, the Harrison. We were the first restaurant to open in Tribeca after 9/11. It became a beacon where so many neighbors and New Yorkers sought solace, connection, and community through our food. Big love at its peak. This spice mix is my signature funk and flavor on the Little Owl Bacon Cheeseburger (page 51) and my Curried Leek Home Fries (page 100).

Salt

Salt is one of the most vital ingredients in the kitchen, but it is grossly taken for granted. I use kosher salt for cooking because it sticks to food better and Maldon sea salt as a finishing salt for its delicate flakes that enhance a dish rather than overpower it. And I can't impress upon you enough how important it is to generously salt your pasta water so that you can season your pasta. I prefer fine sea salt for that job. It has just the right level of saltiness that makes the difference between a pasta dish that makes you want to sing and one that falls flat. Your pasta water should be "salty like the sea," that old kitchen adage. As a guideline, I recommend 2 Tbsp fine sea salt per 1 lb [455 g] pasta.

THE HARRISON SPICE MIX

2 cups [480 g] kosher salt

2 Tbsp Madras curry powder

2 Tbsp cayenne pepper

Combine all the ingredients and store in an airtight container for up to 3 months. Just a pinch or two is dyno-mite!

Wines and Vinegars

Cooking wines found on the grocery store shelf are filled with additives and are of such poor quality that you would never want to drink them. So why would you cook with them? The alcohol burns off in the cooking process and the flavor profile of the wine becomes part of the dish, so think quality, enjoyable wines. I cook with dry, crisp Italian or French white wines, like Pinot Grigio, Chablis, or Sauvignon Blanc. Avoid buttery or oaky American Chardonnay for cooking, as it shows up in the dish. And reach for an excellent dry Italian red wine, like Chianti. An added advantage when choosing a good wine for a recipe is that you can pour yourself a glass while you cook!

Dry vermouth is used for my Littleneck Clams with Juicy Bread (page 168) and Spaghetti and Clams (page 107). And since it keeps for a long time in the refrigerator once opened, you can save it to make a martini. Or just use it as a substitute for white wine in any recipe. A nutty, Sicilian Marsala is terrific to have on hand and is integral to making my super-duper Veal Marsala (page 157). And because you are sharp, you're going to buy a good one! Which means you can whip up a little tiramisu with it or kick back and drink it after dinner one night. For desserts, an excellent dark rum is needed for my Birthday Rum Cake (page 238). It's not a party if somebody isn't a little giggly from their cake. And choose your favorite fine brandy for making my shortcut version of Brandied Cherry and Apple Strudel (page 259) that even Arnold Schwarzenegger would love.

I like to think of vinaigrettes as the sixth mother sauce (see "My Mother Sauce," page 69), and sherry vinegar, which is a touch sweeter and much softer than red wine vinegar, is what I use for my very versatile Sherry Shallot Vinaigrette (page 69). You'll want to make a big batch of this and keep it in your refrigerator, where it will keep for up to two weeks. It's a delicious and beautiful dressing that is used on its own in my Sunflower Salad with Golden Beets (page 74) as well as spun into a marinade and base for several other vinaigrettes throughout *Big Love Cooking*.

Rice wine vinegar is my go-to for quick pickled vegetables. And have somebody treat you to a bottle of aged balsamic vinegar. Look for the words *Traditional Balsamic Vinegar di Modena* along with a red stamp on the bottle to signify the authentic stuff, which is unctuous and sweet (and very expensive!). Dragging a shard of Parmigiano-Reggiano through a few drops of this liquid gold is a classy way to end a meal. A less expensive store-bought balsamic vinegar, however, works great for my Warm Radicchio, Pancetta, and Gorgonzola (page 79). Through the reduction process, it will mimic the syrupy texture of the superior aged balsamic and save you some money.

Oils

Unless otherwise noted, I use extra-virgin olive oil for finishing dishes. And because everyone always asks, the oil that you find on your table at Little Owl is Gerbino organic extra-virgin olive oil, from brothers Gunther and Klaus Di Giovanna in Sicily—the same family that makes our Little Owl Rosso red wine. I use olive oil for cooking at low temperatures. For frying and cooking with high heat, 10 percent blended oil (90 percent vegetable oil, 10 percent olive oil), which is commonly referred to as a neutral cooking oil, is best. Be sure to keep all of your oil stored in a cool, dark place to prevent them from going rancid. Heat and light destroy oils. That means far away from the stove and off a sunny countertop. And let's talk about truffle oil: I use drops of this heady, aromatized oil for truffle vinaigrette. You can drizzle it on asparagus and eggs or even over toasted bread. But if you are going to use truffle oil, I think it is best to skip the grocery store and purchase truffle products from a reputable online purveyor like D'Artagnan.

Cheeses

For my all-star Italian lineup, freshly grated Parmesan is called for throughout these recipes. Please don't buy the inferior commercial version that is already grated. There is no love in that cheese, only caking agents. Some recipes call for pecorino, which is a sheep's milk cheese with a sharper flavor I prefer for finishing many of my pasta dishes. Grana Padano is a less complex and less expensive cow's milk cheese. Fresh ricotta cheese is used for the Ricotta Cavatelli with Tomato Broth, Bacon, and Fava Beans (page 117), and in my house we always had some in the refrigerator. My dad would top any red sauce pasta dish with a dollop of fresh ricotta. For a delightful and easy gnocchi, use fresh goat cheese as a quick base for a luscious sauce. Gorgonzola is an Italian blue cheese that is spicy, salty, and strong. And when it meets the sweetness of the balsamic and the fatty punch of pancetta in my warm radicchio salad, it's a divine combo. Spanish Cabrales is a great blue cheese

alternative for Italian Gorgonzola. Keep some Italian mascarpone and Philadelphia cream cheese in your refrigerator, specifically for two of my favorite South Philly desserts: Birthday Rum Cake (page 238) and Philly Cheesecake with Blueberry Agave Sauce (page 255). Gruyère and fontina are excellent melting cheeses and serve as the bubbly topping to my Onion Soup Gratin (page 61). When choosing an American Cheddar for your burger, look for Wisconsin Cheddar at the store, because their slogan is "Wisconsin Cheddar—nobody does it better." I second that. And while technically not a cheese, crème fraîche is a very high-fat French cultured cream that makes sauces smooth and creamy.

Sauces and Pastes

Sambal chili paste is an Indonesian spicy paste with a base of chile peppers. I use it in several dishes to add heat. Look for it in the Asian section of your grocery store. Once opened, store in it the refrigerator. Oyster sauce, a savory Asian brown sauce, adds "ohh-yum!" to my Sesame Green Beans with Mint, Chile, and Oyster Sauce (page 90). And please, I would never strap you with a laborious restaurant recipe like veal demi-glace (which can take up to 4 days to make), but I do have to tell you that it is the secret to adding a meaty depth of flavor to a dish or sauce. You can purchase store-bought veal demi-glace and it will work well.

Nuts, Seeds, and Dried Fruit

Pine nuts are the base of each pesto recipe, and sesame seed–topped bread from Sarcone's Bakery in South Philly was always on our table. Turn slider buns into sesame seed breadsticks by coating them with toasted sesame seeds. Slivered almonds are a pleasurable crunch in salads as well as in several of my desserts. Sunflower seeds say, "Hello, summer!" while pumpkin seeds usher in the fall and elevate Broccoli, Cauliflower, and Mushrooms with Pepita Salsa Verde (page 87). And have some dried cherries and dried cranberries on hand to add tartness and sweetness to salads and desserts.

Bread

Japanese panko bread crumbs are all I use for my meatballs. And in dessert. And on salads. And everywhere! I love them. And they don't take up a lot of space. Buy the unseasoned, plain variety and make Panko Crunchies (see page 78) for a textural topper on a pasta dish, or add them to my Little Gem Caesar (page 78) for a crouton feel without breaking a tooth (large, hard croutons are the worst). An excellent baguette is recommended for slicing, toasting, and spreading with Chicken Liver Mousse (page 140) or any number of quick crostini. I also love a crusty baguette to dip in Sunday Gravy (page 211) for bread n' gravy when no one is looking. And for my School Days Sausage and Peppers Sandwiches (page 49), use excellent store-bought sesame seed Kaiser rolls—you need something to hold up to the delicious juices once you take a bite. The secret to my Brioche French Toast with Stewed Strawberries (page 35) is brioche bread that has a high egg and butter content, making it dense and rich and fabulous.

Canned Tomatoes

Buy San Marzano whole peeled canned tomatoes. You can squish them right into the pot, or just let them sit and simmer for a long time and break down in my Simple Marinara (page 106), which, by the way, is a huge part of big love cooking. You can use marinara as a flavorful addition to vegetables or as a base for pasta, and it's the secret to a fast and easy Italian Fish Stew (page 193). Stock up on tomato paste, the thick, richly concentrated paste in a tiny can—just a spoonful is excellent for adding to marinara to make a crazy-good South Philly–style thick and sweet Mom-Mom Pizza Sauce (page 43).

Pasta and Seafood

Let's talk garnishing seafood pasta dishes with cheese: Just do it. I do! It's delicious. OK, done.

BIG LOVE COOKING ESSENTIALS

The most important but simple, old-school kitchen gadgets that I use at home and at Little Owl are my own hands, a food mill, and a fine-mesh sieve. Clean hands are always your best tool. Use best practices and clean and dry your hands thoroughly between touching each ingredient, and you shouldn't have any issues. When called for, use tongs. They are also great for lifting long pastas right out of the pot and into the pan to finish and emulsify with sauce.

A food mill separates skins and seeds and is an indispensable tool for achieving a smooth texture for tomato gravy. A fine-mesh sieve comes in handy for sifting flour and creating purées or straining stocks. I even use one to create a light-as-air texture for my Chicken Liver Mousse (page 140). They come in different sizes for tasks large and small.

To get the most fragrant and powerful flavor, use a spice grinder to grind your own spices from whole seeds whenever possible. Just don't use your coffee grinder for grinding spices and vice versa. Keep them separate.

Moving on to more modern conveniences that are the mainstay of my commercial and home kitchens: A KitchenAid mixer with a hook attachment is perfect for working dough. And while I rely on the old workhorse Robot Coupe food processor, which chops and grinds like nobody's business, KitchenAid is the better-known brand for the home cook, and I recommend that or Cuisinart. Keep in mind, I don't like grating fresh cheese in a food processor. Any friction that is generated by the blade simply destroys the cheese. It deserves more. So, whenever possible, gently grate fresh cheeses with a box grater. Or double down on the use of a Microplane grater for zesting lemons or

grating fresh horseradish and use it to grate hard cheeses as well.

For kitchen knives, I recommend that you keep it simple. With these four knives, you can accomplish any kitchen task: a chef's knife (8 to 10 in [20 to 25 cm] blade), a serrated knife, a paring knife, and a boning knife for cutting around skin and bones on fish and meat, and especially for deboning a whole chicken to make the Little Owl Crispy Chicken (page 146). Yes! I'll take you through the steps to chicken heaven. And speaking of sharp objects, a kitchen mandoline is wonderful for slicing fruits and vegetables for pickling or shaving into a salad.

When preparing to cook, keep several sizes of mixing bowls at the ready. They can be glass, aluminum, or plastic. Look for bowls that can also double as airtight containers with lids. Ladles are essential for spooning soups and sauces, and I recommend you have a variety of sizes, with 4 oz [118 ml], 6 oz [177 ml], and 8 oz [236 ml] being the most practical for home use. And a slotted spoon is important for lifting meats out of gravy, as well as Cinnamon Sugar Beignets (page 36) out of hot oil. And if you have only one spatula in your kitchen, by far the most versatile is a fish spatula. It's great for lifting fish fillets out of a pan or broiler, and its fluted head makes it excellent for flipping pancakes or burgers, too.

The pasta section of *Big Love Cooking* is ample and features my Ricotta Cavatelli (page 117), so now is your time to pick up a hand-crank cavatelli cutter. Priced under $30, this easy-to-use tool will make you the cavatelli-making queen (or king) in your neighborhood, like I am in mine. "Homemades" (page 221), my grandmother's homemade tagliatelle, are easy to make with a pasta maker and you can purchase a basic, hand-crank one for around $40.

For Sunday supper (or most meals any day of the week), you'll want a bevy of kitchen towels and wooden spoons. Also, for rolling out dough, I recommend a heavy, wooden dowel roller without handles. It should do the work of flattening the dough for you, and the handle-less kind will feel more like an extension of your hands as you roll. Never put wooden spoons or a wooden rolling pin in the dishwasher, as it will destroy them. The same goes for any wooden cutting boards. You will want to reserve one large wooden cutting board for pasta making. If you don't have one, you can use a clean, dry surface, like your kitchen table. And you'll need smaller boards for chopping.

For draining pasta, use a stainless steel colander. You can also use it to wash and rinse vegetables.

I do not have a pastry chef at Little Owl, preferring instead to make my own homemade desserts. My mission is simple: I want preparing and eating dessert to make you happy. Baking is kitchen science. And while I am not a molecular gastronomist, following exact measurements ensures the success of a recipe. And with that success comes the confidence to try new things in the kitchen. Dry measuring cups do not reflect true volume measurements, and as such do not correspond to liquid measures. A standard set of dry measuring cups should include ¼ cup [60 ml], ⅓ cup [80 ml], ½ cup [125 ml], and 1 cup [250 ml] scoops. In addition to dry measuring cups, I recommend the use of a digital scale for measuring dry ingredients like flour and sugar by weight. And make

sure you are at eye level with the markers on a simple Pyrex glass or plastic measuring cup when measuring liquid ingredients to ensure an accurate measurement. And on the topic of accurate measurements, an instant-read thermometer is a great tool for checking the doneness of meats. Some of these things are best done by sight and touch, but if you are wary of your food being at a certain temperature, use one.

Offset spatulas are great for evening out cake batter and spreading frosting, and a pastry bag comes in handy for spreading pastry cream (or make your own by filling a large zip-top baggie and snipping off a corner). Among all the available kitchen whisks on the market, look for a simple all-purpose French whisk for everything from beating eggs to whipping cream. Parchment paper, plastic wrap, and large zip-top baggies for storage also top my list as prep items and they should be in a drawer close by.

Cooling racks aren't just for fresh-from-the-oven cakes; they are also for cooling meats. Stainless steel rimmed baking sheets are just as great for baking cookies as they are for roasting vegetables or toasting nuts.

In terms of serving food, think family style. Beautiful, funky plates and dishes make everyone feel good. I love to serve wine in "Uncle Frankie" glasses (little juice glasses that I pick up at Fishs Eddy in Manhattan), named after my Uncle Frankie, who drank his wine this way. If there is one thing I love to do at home, it's to plate food on beautiful platters and pass it around. Or just park it in the center of the table with complementary items on the side. Think abbondanza—plentiful portions that can be parlayed into leftovers or spun into other meals.

CHAPTER 1

Brunch

Brunch

On New York City weekends, *brunching* is a verb and a ritual: a simple, much-needed pleasure of just being together over good food after a long week. And every neighborhood has its own unique rhythm. Sightseeing, selfies, and brunching underscores our little West Village world on the corner of Bedford and Grove. Young, transient neighbors haul laundry up our gorgeous block, peppered with iconic New York City fire escapes, dodging a worldly mix of tourists who have come to see the *Friends* building (our Little Owl building at 90 Bedford Street is the establishing shot for the TV show's impossibly *large* apartment).

But there are *real* history and *real* friends on our block. We have the secret alley of Grove Court—a collection of tiny townhouses from the 1850s set back from the street to shame and hide the poor but which are now looked on with longing. We have the narrowest house in New York City at 75½ Bedford, where poet Edna St. Vincent Millay once lived. We have Marie's Crisis, a beloved basement-level piano bar on Grove Street where Thomas Paine died (it's revolutionary). And of course,

17 Grove Street: a rare wooden home, with its beautiful owl on top, to which we owe our name. There are so many others who also make a home (or feel at home) on Bedford and Grove. Some of these Little Owl friends have a sublime love story; a day-old bag of Dunkin' Donuts for our staff each night; a beloved mother in Queens who stuffs one hundred shells from Raffetto's on Christmas Eve; a claim to have drunk Frank Sinatra under the table; a treasured wit and character; a tipsy wave for us through the window; the nickname "Bud"; and a penchant for Cinnamon Sugar Beignets (page 36), strong coffee, and a Little Owl Bacon Cheeseburger (page 51) on the weekend. And *all of them* have a big love vibe beyond compare. Our little corner is enchanting.

But without ever setting foot on our block or inside Little Owl, you can re-create some of our magic in your kitchen. Call the whole gang over for the big game and bust out some School Days Sausage and Peppers Sandwiches (page 49). Wow them with Little Owl Gravy Meatball Sliders (page 226), too, while you're at it!

Whole Wheat Pancakes

with Berries **33**

Brioche French Toast

with Stewed Strawberries **35**

Cinnamon Sugar Beignets

with Raspberry Sauce and Nutella **36**

Parmesan Asparagus 'n' a Egg **41**

Mom-Mom Pizza **42**

Fontina Sausage Biscuits **45**

Fontina Sausage Biscuits

with Poached Eggs, Italian Greens, and Hollandaise **46**

School Days Sausage and Peppers Sandwiches **49**

Little Owl Bacon Cheeseburger **51**

THE BIRDHOUSES OF GROVE STREET

Richard Eric Weigle, the president of the Grove Street Block Association, continually looks for ways to improve the appearance and quality of life on Grove Street. He works with the NYPD's Sixth Precinct to lower crime, as well as with local businesses and residents to beautify the street in every way we can. One night, he told me he had a dream that Grove Street became known not only for its historical, quaint houses and tree-lined blocks, but also as the street with the beautiful birdhouses! He and his husband, Michael Anastasio, already had a small collection of birdhouses, but after his dream, friends from Amsterdam and around the country started donating more birdhouses to turn his vision into a reality. More than a dozen birdhouses strategically hung on Grove Street add a homey, almost rural vibe to our block. During bleak New York City winters, their red birdhouses add a pop of joy and color to our world. And all kinds of birds are welcome—as are people of all races, religions, and sexual orientations—symbolizing the tolerant, welcoming vibe that has always been our Greenwich Village.

BEDFORD STREET,
A.K.A. LARRY SELMAN WAY

For 50 years, until his passing in 2013, Bedford Street was the home of disabled neighbor and friend, Larry Selman. Mentally challenged, yet living independently, since 1978 Larry spent his days selflessly collecting money for multiple charities and selling raffle tickets for the Bedford Barrow Commerce Block Association. He was an altruistic activist whose limitations were surpassed by his grand spirit. He was a fixture in the neighborhood and a friend of Little Owl. In her Academy Award–nominated short documentary film, *The Collector of Bedford Street*, director Alice Elliott tells the story of how Larry's compassionate neighbors came to his aid when he was faced with eviction. In 2013, a street sign with the honorific *Larry Selman Way* was bestowed on Bedford Street to commemorate his place in our neighborhood. He was one of many folks on our block who inspired the best in us. A neighborhood joint isn't there to just feed your belly—it should also feed your spirit. And with Little Owl, I wanted to celebrate relationships—yours and ours—and treat people well with this in mind. It's not just hospitable, it's human.

WHOLE WHEAT PANCAKES
with Berries

Alton Brown loves these pancakes, calling them the best *cake* he's ever had! He's right! Pancakes are still a cake. You bake one and you griddle the other. Top these with a naturally sweet combo of strawberries and blueberries, or my favorite: raspberries! Or the end of summer may bring juicy blackberries to your part of the world. If you happen to get your hands on tiny, wild blueberries, gently fold them right into the mix after it rests for an intense berry burst in each bite. You might be surprised to hear this, but don't put butter or oil on your cooking surface before making your pancakes. For the very best results, start with a dry, hot, nonstick surface. The batter already has butter in it, and that will help create a perfectly caramelized, evenly cooked outside that lightly crisps and protects a fluffy, cake texture inside. Getting rid of funky, uneven brown patches on the bottom of your pancakes never felt so good!

In a large bowl, combine both flours, the sugar, baking soda, baking powder, and salt and whisk to combine. Crack the egg into small bowl, add the milk and melted butter, and whisk until the mixture is well combined. Pour the milk mixture into the flour mixture and use a wooden spoon to mix just enough to make a homogenous batter. Do not overmix! Overmixing dry flour with wet ingredients is what develops the flour's gluten. This will make your pancakes tough. Rocky Balboa is tough. Pancakes shouldn't be.

Let the mixture rest for 10 minutes so that the gluten in the flour has time to relax, yielding a more tender pancake.

Preheat your electric griddle to 375°F [190°C]. Or you can pre-heat a nonstick sauté pan or skillet over medium heat.

cont.

1 cup [140 g] whole wheat flour

½ cup [70 g] all-purpose flour

1 Tbsp sugar

1 Tbsp baking soda

2 tsp baking powder

¼ tsp kosher salt

1 egg

1 cup [240 ml] whole milk

3 Tbsp unsalted butter, melted, plus ½ cup [110 g] butter, for serving

Pure New York maple syrup (or your favorite), for serving

⅓ cup [45 g] fresh strawberries, stemmed, hulled, and sliced

⅓ cup [45 g] fresh blueberries

Pour the batter onto the griddle in ¼ cup [60 ml] increments. A 2 oz [60 ml] ladle works great here! Form pancakes about 4 in [10 cm] wide, leaving enough space between them so that they fit comfortably on the griddle—about 2 in [5 cm] is best. Nothing beautiful is ever perfect, so don't worry about pouring perfectly round circles onto the pan. (Sometimes I like to drizzle the batter into letters and shapes—it's the kid in me.)

Cook the pancakes on one side until you see bubbles form on the surface in the middle of the pancake (not just at the edges) and the underside is a uniform golden brown, about 2 minutes. Use a thin spatula to flip and cook on the other side until golden brown, too, about 1 minute more.

Transfer the cooked pancakes to a platter, stacking them with pats of butter in between. Continue cooking until you have used all of your batter. Serve the pancakes immediately with your favorite maple syrup and the strawberries and blueberries on the side.

BRIOCHE FRENCH TOAST
with Stewed Strawberries

The secret to my Little Owl French toast starts with an excellent brioche bread. Truly, no other bread will give you that rich, knock-your-socks-off, decadent pastry taste than a brioche loaf (I get mine from Amy's Bread in Manhattan—they make the best!). The high egg and butter content of brioche make this French toast taste like dessert, and regulars at Little Owl often share one after a meal for a sweet finish. However, if you are unable to get your hands on a fresh baked brioche loaf, don't despair! Store-bought packaged brioche buns or rolls also work great. Note that a slightly stale brioche works best for this recipe. And since you won't be using an entire loaf for this recipe, you can preslice any remaining brioche and store the slices for up to 1 week in your freezer for later use.

To make the strawberries: In a small saucepan over low heat, combine the strawberries, sugar, lemon juice, and cinnamon sticks. Cook until the strawberries release their juices and soften, about 10 minutes. Set aside to cool. Remove and discard the cinnamon sticks before serving.

To make the French toast: In a large, shallow bowl, combine the egg yolks, milk, heavy cream, sugar, and vanilla and whisk until the sugar is completely dissolved.

Preheat an electric griddle to 350°F [180°C] or a cast-iron skillet set over medium-high heat and add 2 Tbsp of the butter, letting it melt to coat the griddle.

Working one at a time, dip the brioche slices in the egg mixture, coating each side. Stay awake, sleepyhead! Brioche is very soft and will soak up the mixture right away—in less than 30 seconds. Immediately transfer a soaked slice to the hot griddle and cook until the underside is golden brown, about 2 minutes. Use a spatula to flip and cook 2 minutes more, until the flipped side is golden brown, too. Add the remaining 2 Tbsp of butter, letting it melt to recoat the griddle and repeat the process with the remaining slices, dipping and then cooking as many slices at once that will fit comfortably on your griddle. Distribute the cooked slices among four plates and generously spoon the stewed strawberries on top. Serve immediately.

SERVES 4

Stewed Strawberries

2 cups [280 g] strawberries, stemmed, hulled, and quartered

¼ cup [50 g] sugar

1 Tbsp fresh lemon juice

2 cinnamon sticks

French Toast

6 egg yolks (reserve the whites for an egg wash, omelet, or meringue)

2 cups [480 ml] whole milk

1½ cups [360 ml] heavy cream

⅓ cup [65 g] sugar

1 tsp vanilla extract

4 Tbsp unsalted butter, for cooking

Brioche loaf, cut into eight ¾ in [2 cm] thick slices, or 4 store-bought brioche rolls, split in half

SFINGE, ZEPPOLE, PIZZA FRITTA, AND BOMBOLONI, OH MAMA MIA!

Since Little Owl doesn't scream *Italian-American*, I snuck these little dough-nuts onto the menu and called them beignets. But here's the skinny on these goodies: my beignet recipe is really an eggless twist on four similar popular fried treats. New Orleans beignets are true to their French origin and begin with a choux pastry dough. *Sfinge*, popular in Sicily and also found in my hometown at the 9th Street Italian Market, sometimes include ricotta cheese in the dough. After frying, they are filled with custard cream and topped with a cherry. You'll see these served in old-school New York pastry shops like Veniero's in the East Village or Rocco's on Bleecker Street. *Pizza fritta* are popular among Neapolitan families: Just take leftover pizza dough, fry it, and dust it with powdered sugar—that's really the inspiration for my take on beignets. Fried dough. No egg. *Pizza fritta* is popular on Fat Tuesday or Martedì Grasso, to mark the last hurrah before the Lenten season fast begins. And then we have *zeppole*. Just about every street festival in New York has a *zeppole* stall. These delicious, fried balls have become synonymous with Italian doughnuts, and they are what my beignets most closely resemble. While *pizza fritta* tends to be puffy and square, *zeppole* take on the look of a doughnut hole. While we're at it, *zeppole* closely resemble *bomboloni* (Italian for "doughnuts"), which are usually filled with a raspberry jam. Regardless of what you want to call them, here's what I think: Fried dough and sugar plus Nutella equals love.

MAKES 14 TO 16 BEIGNETS

Raspberry Sauce

2 cups [240 g] fresh raspberries

½ cup [120 ml] red wine

2 tsp sugar

1 cinnamon stick

Beignets

½ cup [100 g] sugar

2 tsp ground cinnamon

¾ cup [180 ml] whole milk

1 Tbsp molasses

1⅛ oz fresh yeast

cont.

CINNAMON SUGAR BEIGNETS
with Raspberry Sauce and Nutella

I love the look, the smell, and the feeling of nostalgia that these beignets evoke: They might remind you of carnivals or street fairs or warm dough-nuts from your childhood on a snowy day. In my family, these are simply called "fried dough," and as kids, we would go nuts over them. My Little Owl version of beignets are round, dusted with cinnamon sugar, plopped onto smears of Italian Nutella, then drizzled with homemade raspberry sauce—a departure from the expected Café Du Monde New Orleans–style beignet. When we first opened, I piped a raspberry filling inside the beig-nets like *bomboloni*. But no one loves raspberries as much as me, so serving it drizzled on the top or on the side for dipping is just as dreamy, too.

To make the raspberry sauce: In a medium saucepan over medium-low heat, combine the raspberries, red wine, sugar, and cinnamon stick and cook, stirring frequently to crush the berries into the liquid until it comes to a gentle boil, 3 to 5 minutes. Discard the cinnamon stick and use an immersion blender to blend into a smooth sauce. Set aside.

To make the beignets: In a small bowl, combine the sugar and cinnamon and mix well. Set aside. Line a large plate with paper towels and set aside.

In a small saucepan over low heat, warm the milk until it reaches 105°F [40°C]. If you don't have a thermometer, just know that you should be able to comfortably stick your finger in it.

In the bowl of a stand mixer with the dough hook attachment, add the warmed milk, molasses, and yeast and on low speed, stir to combine, about 1 minute.

Add 1 cup [140 g] of the flour and the melted butter, increase the speed to medium, and mix until just combined, scraping down the sides to incorporate the flour as necessary. Gradually add the remaining 1 cup [140 g] of flour and mix until a soft, smooth dough forms, about 1 minute.

Turn off the mixer and drape the top of the mixing bowl with a moist, clean kitchen towel (mom-mom style) or cover with plastic wrap. Place the bowl in a warm spot on your counter until the dough rises and doubles in size, about 30 minutes.

Once the dough rises, it will be soft, elastic, and slightly sticky to the touch. Gently turn it out onto a lightly floured surface. Sprinkle a pinch or two more flour on top to make it less sticky and begin to pinch off 1 oz [30 g] balls of dough by squeezing the dough between your pointer finger and thumb. (You can weigh or eyeball your dough balls—it's not an exact science here, but you'll be looking to yield between 14 and 16 beignets.)

Slap the dough ball down onto your floured surface and, using a bit of pressure, roll it into a smooth ball. Repeat squeezing off dough balls and rolling, setting them 2 in [5 cm] apart on a baking sheet until you've pinched and rolled all the dough. Cover the baking sheet tightly with plastic wrap and return them to your warm spot to rise again, about 10 minutes.

cont.

2 cups [280 g] all-purpose flour

1 Tbsp unsalted butter, melted

3 cups [720 ml] or more neutral oil, such as canola or vegetable, for frying

¼ cup [75 g] Nutella chocolate hazelnut spread, for serving

Meanwhile, in a large Dutch oven or heavy pot over medium-high heat, add 3 cups [720 ml] (or more, if necessary) neutral oil to a depth of 3 in [7.5 cm] and heat until it reaches 350°F [180°C]. Use a thermometer to measure the temperature or drop a beignet in the oil—if the dough begins to crisp and sizzle, you're in business!

Working in batches of 4 to 6 at a time (depending on the size of your pot—you don't want to overcrowd them), place the beignets in the hot oil and fry. They will bob up and down in the oil as they cook and get your house smelling yeasty and sweet. Turn them often, frying evenly on all sides until golden, 3 to 4 minutes.

Use a slotted spoon to transfer the beignets to the prepared plate to drain for a moment before rolling each one in the cinnamon sugar. Pile them high on a serving platter along with the Nutella and raspberry sauce on the side for dipping. Serve immediately.

PARMESAN ASPARAGUS 'N' A EGG

When we had leftover asparagus in the spring or summertime, my mom-mom would say, "Joe, ya' want some asparagus 'n' a egg?" I can still hear her describing every dish she made as "something n' something." And the way I write my menu at Little Owl is an ode to my South Philly childhood and the way I remember hearing my mom-mom's food. I can't get it out of my ear, nor do I want to! Note: By blanching the asparagus spears first, you'll get them tender-crisp and lock in a bright green color that won't fade when you finish them in the oven just enough to cook "a egg."

Preheat the oven to 350°F [180°C].

Prepare an ice water bath by filling a large bowl (preferably metal) with cold water and ice cubes. Set aside.

Bring a large pot of generously salted water to a boil. Add the asparagus and boil until they turn a bright green color and are tender, 3 to 4 minutes. Using tongs, remove the asparagus and plunge them into the ice water bath, and let sit for about 1 minute. Pull them out of the water, pat dry, and transfer to a mixing bowl. Add the olive oil, and using your hands, toss the asparagus until well coated.

Transfer the asparagus to a baking sheet and divide them into groups of 4 spears each, allowing a little space between the spears to support the egg yolk. Using your fingers, top each group of spears with a generous mound of Parmesan cheese, creating a small nest for the egg yolk. Gently place each egg yolk on a mound of cheese, season with a few grinds of black pepper, and bake until the yolks are just set, 3 to 4 minutes.

Transfer each asparagus and egg group to a plate and sprinkle a few flakes of Maldon sea salt right in the center of the yolk. Get them pretty with a pop of pink by scattering the red onions across the top. Let it rain Panko Crunchies all over until you use them up and garnish with your pick of lettuces, if using. Drizzle with extra-virgin olive oil and serve immediately.

SERVES 4

16 spears fresh medium-thick asparagus, tough ends trimmed and discarded

1 Tbsp olive oil

½ cup [50 g] finely grated fresh Parmesan cheese

4 egg yolks (reserve the whites for an egg wash, omelet, or meringue)

Freshly ground black pepper

Maldon sea salt

¼ cup [50 g] drained Pickled Red Onions (page 84)

½ cup [30 g] Panko Crunchies (see page 78)

A small handful of frisée, chicory, or curly endive (optional)

Extra-virgin olive oil, for drizzling

IT'S YOUR JAWN Once you bake a Mom-Mom Pizza, it's your *jawn* (pronounced *JHAO-N*, South Philly speak for "it's your thing"). And you can do any number of things with it! Right before baking, add fresh mozzarella and enjoy it hot and gooey. Try it with sliced avocado, Maldon sea salt flakes, and grinds of black pepper for Italian-style avocado toast. It's so yummy topped with Tender Broccoli Rabe and Toasted Garlic (page 93) or Sautéed Escarole (page 233). Want to experience total heaven? Blanket a slice with Caramelized Onions (see page 61). Once cool, top it with olive oil–packed Italian tuna tossed with Pepper-Fennel Relish (page 188). Try it the Little Owl brunch way: Cut a large slice of room-temperature Mom-Mom Pizza and top it with a fried egg, a few paper-thin slices of prosciutto, and some fresh arugula drizzled with olive oil. For the record, I am not the kind of chef who thinks everything tastes better with an egg on it. But I do enjoy giving people what they want. And I've learned *anything* topped with an egg is exactly what people want! The beauty of a slice of Mom-Mom Pizza is that it tastes amazing at room temperature, which makes it a terrific vehicle for all sorts of toppings that you can riff on for breakfast, lunch, or dinner. (This pizza is a "mom-mom" kind of love—all give.)

MOM-MOM PIZZA

SERVES 8

2 packets active dry yeast

¼ cup [60 ml] olive oil

2 Tbsp molasses

1 Tbsp finely chopped fresh oregano, or 1 tsp dried oregano

2 tsp kosher salt

4 cups [560 g] all-purpose flour

¾ cup [180 ml] Mom-Mom Pizza Sauce (recipe follows), or more as needed

½ cup [30 g] finely grated pecorino cheese

"Mom-Mom" is what I called my grandmother Rosie Bova, and she worked wonders with pizza. She employed two simple secrets. The first is that she used a cast-iron sheet tray, which holds and distributes heat better than a run-of-the-mill aluminum cookie sheet and gives you that wonderful, golden-brown crispy crust on the bottom and on the edges of the pizza. The second is she put oregano in the dough, giving it a whisper of an herb flavor. And my third, additional secret is to use molasses instead of sugar to provide a depth of flavor and a toasty brown color, too! That crispy olive oil underside and soft, gooey layer on top where the sauce meets the dough make it distinctly South Philly. And the best part is that this pizza tastes brilliant at room temperature, which means you can make it hours ahead of time. Note: I recommend using a 12¼ by 18¼ in [31 by 46.5 cm] sheet tray and cutting your pizza into sixteen 4 in [10 cm] squares—but have some fun with it and cut it into any size that floats your boat. (But 4 in [10 cm] squares further divide into little triangles that are perfect for Mom-Mom pizza party bites, just saying!)

Brush a large mixing bowl with olive oil. Set aside.

In a stand mixer with the hook attachment, add the yeast, 1½ cups [360 ml] of warm water, the olive oil, molasses, oregano, and salt and mix on low speed until combined, about 1 minute. With the mixer running, add the flour and continue mixing until a dough ball forms around the hook. Transfer the dough ball to the prepared mixing bowl and cover with plastic wrap. Place the bowl in a warm spot on your counter until the dough rises and doubles in size, about 1 hour.

Preheat the oven to 500°F [260°C].

Turn the dough out onto a lightly floured surface and sprinkle a scant amount of flour on top. Using a rolling pin, gently roll it out to the shape of your pan. Transfer the dough to the baking sheet and, using your fingertips, punch it down and stretch it out so that it is evenly distributed and has a uniform thickness, about ¼ in [6 mm] thick.

Using a large spoon, spread a thin, even layer of Mom-Mom Pizza Sauce over the dough, leaving a 1 in [2.5 cm] border of uncovered dough along the edges. Use about ¾ cup [180 ml] sauce to cover the pizza (or more, if you like more). Whatever you do not use can be reserved for another pizza. Set the pizza aside, uncovered in a warm place, and let rise again before baking, about 10 minutes.

Sprinkle the pecorino over the pizza and bake for 12 minutes. Let cool to room temperature before cutting and serving plain (the old-school way), or see "It's Your Jawn" (facing page) for topping ideas.

MOM-MOM PIZZA SAUCE

This pizza sauce is thick, sweet, and so fast to make. If you do not have my Simple Marinara (page 106) on hand, you can use a store-bought marinara for faster prep time.

MAKES 1¼ CUPS [300 ML]

1 cup [240 ml] Simple Marinara (page 106)

¼ cup [70 g] tomato paste

1 Tbsp sugar

In a small saucepan over medium-high heat, add the marinara, tomato paste, and sugar. Using a wooden spoon, stir to combine. Bring to a boil, then lower the heat and simmer for 5 minutes. Done.

LET'S TALK HANDMADE BISCUITS

Pull up a chair.
I need to talk to you about making biscuits.

Working hands-on with biscuits is the best way to ensure they will be light and flaky. Don't be tempted to use a stand mixer (I see that look in your eye that is hoping for a shortcut!). The rapid whirring of a stand mixer generates heat, which in turn creates friction that melts the butter. And we don't want that! We want to keep the butter very cold—don't even take it out of the refrigerator until the moment you absolutely need it, which is right when you're ready to cut it into the flour mixture. The cold butter and the fat from the sausage and cheese will melt while baking, and it is to this alchemy that biscuits owe their tender flakes. Since I think our hands are the best tool in the kitchen, you can cut in the butter, sausage, and cheese and also mix in the buttermilk by hand. But it's very messy! (When cutting in the butter, use just your fingertips, as they are less warm than your palms and so there is less risk of melting the butter in the process.) Or, you can also achieve a great result by using a pastry cutter to cut the ingredients into the flour. Take your pick. Also, whichever method you choose, please note that when working with the dough, be tender and gentle; don't slam it around. You just want to get the butter, sausage, and cheese incorporated and the biscuits formed as quickly as possible. Because of the addition of the sausage and cheese, the yield on these biscuits with a standard 3 in [7.5 cm] biscuit cutter is about 18 biscuits (especially if you gather up your scraps to roll out that last biscuit, which I want you to do! Leave no dough behind!). If you aren't planning on baking them to eat all at once, place them on a baking sheet, cover with plastic wrap, and freeze. Once frozen, transfer to an airtight container and store in your freezer for up to 1 week until ready to use. Before baking, allow as many as you like to thaw in the refrigerator before following the baking directions. You can split these biscuits open and fill them with *your* favorite brunch sandwich fixings, like more sausage, avocado, or salami and cheese.

I had so much to tell you. Ready?

FONTINA SAUSAGE BISCUITS

MAKES 18 BISCUITS

As a kid, if I was running out of the house on a cold morning, late for school or work, I'd make my way straight to McDonald's to pick up a sausage, egg, and cheese biscuit. These biscuits are my grown-up chef's answer to that childhood indulgence. Little bits of sausage and fontina cheese stud the biscuits throughout, so you can eat them plain and still get that sausage sandwich feel, or you can enjoy them how I like to serve them for brunch at Little Owl: with poached eggs, Italian greens, and hollandaise (page 46). To make the best, flakiest biscuits, follow my handmade biscuit tips (see facing page).

¼ cup [55 g] unsalted butter, plus ½ cup [110 g] cold unsalted butter, cut into ½ in [12 mm] cubes

4 cups [560 g] all-purpose flour

1 Tbsp baking powder

1 tsp kosher salt

1½ cups [360 ml] cold buttermilk

6 oz [170 g] breakfast link sausage, removed from the casing and crumbled, or crumbled sausage patties

4 oz [115 g] fontina cheese, cut into ¼ in [6 mm] cubes

Preheat the oven to 375°F [180°C]. Line a baking sheet with parchment paper.

In a small saucepan over low heat, melt ¼ cup of the butter. Set aside.

In a very large bowl, add the flour, baking powder, and salt and whisk to combine. Add the cold butter and, using your fingertips (or a pastry cutter or, in a pinch, a potato masher!), squeeze the butter pieces into the flour until the texture of the mixture turns crumbly, about 2 minutes. Slowly add the buttermilk and, using your hands or a wooden spoon, incorporate until just combined (it will look a mess!). Add the crumbled sausage and the cheese and, using your hands or a pastry cutter, incorporate the sausage and cheese into the dough.

Turn the biscuit dough out onto a lightly floured work surface and sprinkle the top with a little more flour. Using a rolling pin (the dough shouldn't stick to the pin, but if it does, add a scant amount of flour), gently and quickly roll out the dough to about a 1 in [2.5 cm] thick oval. Pull the dough in around the edges and pat it down into somewhat of a square.

Using a 3 in [7.5 cm] biscuit cutter, punch out the biscuits and place them, with a little space between each one, on your prepared baking sheet. Gather any scrap pieces of dough and reroll to cut out as many biscuits as possible.

Brush the biscuits with the melted butter and bake until the tops are lightly golden, 15 minutes. These are best served immediately, or you can store them in an airtight container for up to 24 hours in your refrigerator. To serve the next day, split them open and arrange them on a baking sheet in a 350°F [180°C] oven and warm, until slightly toasted.

Hollandaise Sauce

2 egg yolks (reserve the
whites for an egg wash,
omelet, or meringue)

1 tsp fresh lemon juice

1 cup [220 g] butter,
melted and hot!

Cayenne pepper

Kosher salt

Poached Eggs

2 Tbsp white wine

8 eggs

4 Fontina Sausage Biscuits
(page 45)

1 recipe Sautéed
Escarole (page 233)

FONTINA SAUSAGE BISCUITS
with Poached Eggs, Italian Greens, and Hollandaise

Hollandaise is an easy, thick, delicious sauce to drip over your poached eggs (it's great over asparagus, too!). There is no magic trick here, just a lot of whisking. Once upon a time, when I was twenty-four years old and "knew everything," I broke the hollandaise (when the eggs and butter separate; it's sad) in the middle of a busy shift with Chef Andrew Humbert at the Universal Grill in the executive dining room on the back lot of Universal Studios. And he fixed it by yelling at me. And having me remake it quickly using melted butter instead of clarified butter. By doing so, the milk solids help emulsify the sauce, giving it a nice body. I haven't gone back to clarified butter since. Thanks, Andrew!

To make the hollandaise: Partially fill a medium saucepan with water and bring to a boil over high heat.

Meanwhile, in a large, stainless steel bowl, combine the egg yolks and lemon juice and whisk continuously, until the bright yellow color pales and the mixture begins to thicken, about 2 minutes.

Lower the heat so that the water in the saucepan is barely simmering (you're just using the residual heat from the boil—otherwise you'll cook the eggs) and place the bowl with the egg and lemon mixture on top to create a double boiler. The bottom of the bowl shouldn't touch the water, it should hover right above it.

Drip in the melted butter, very slowly drippy-dripping it in and whisking until it resembles a hot mayonnaise, about 30 seconds. But you want hollandaise! So, loosen it up by adding 1 Tbsp of hot water from the saucepan, and continue whisking. Pour the remaining hot butter in a slow and steady stream and whisk constantly, until the sauce thickens and its volume doubles, 7 to 8 minutes more. Make it taste killer and whisk in a pinch of cayenne and a pinch of salt. Cover to keep warm until serving. (Psst . . . is your hollandaise too thick? Add another bit of hot water and whisk before serving.)

cont.

To prepare the poached eggs: Fill a large saucepan with water and bring to a boil over high heat. Reduce the heat to a simmer, add the white wine and give the whole thing one vigorous whisk so that the water swirls (not a vortex, mind you—just a swirl). This allows the albumen of the yolk to disperse, which will make your egg look pretty.

Crack one egg at a time into a small bowl and gently slide it into the center of the swirling water. You can fit 4 eggs at once in the saucepan, so work in two batches. Cook until the whites set and the yolks are runny, 3 to 4 minutes.

Meanwhile, split 4 biscuits in half and top each half with some sautéed escarole. Use a slotted spoon to transfer the poached egg to a biscuit half. Repeat with each egg, transferring to the biscuits. Top each egg with warm hollandaise and serve immediately.

SCHOOL DAYS SAUSAGE AND PEPPERS SANDWICHES

Growing up as an Italian-American in South Philly meant that there were three things you could count on: Catholic school, Sunday gravy, and Sunday gravy leftovers for Monday lunch. However, instead of Catholic school, my parents sent me to public school in Center City. I rolled into school most Mondays with my mom's sausage and peppers sandwich on a sesame seed roll in my lunch bag. And most kids thought I was a weirdo. One day, there was a "situation" with another kid. And in my need to diffuse it, I offered him a bite of my sausage and peppers sandwich (he was expecting spice, but instead was hooked on the taste of the sweet, slow-cooked peppers and rich sausage). It was a very eye-opening experience for me; I understood for the first time how to create relationships through food. And also, I understood the power of negotiation. *Aha!* I thought. *Now I can come in with the goods and in return try something I never get at home: peanut butter and jelly on whole wheat bread.*

In a medium heavy pot over medium-high heat, add 2 Tbsp of the olive oil and warm until it shimmers. Add the sausage links and cook, turning now and then to brown on all sides, 8 to 10 minutes (depending on the plumpness of your links). Using tongs, remove the sausage from the pot, transfer to a cutting board, and set aside.

To the same pot, add the remaining 1 Tbsp oil, the peppers, onions, and garlic. Season generously with salt and black pepper, lower the heat to medium, and cook until the peppers and onions are softened, 10 to 12 minutes.

Meanwhile, use a sharp knife to cut each link into ½ in [12 mm] thick diagonal slices. You probably noticed that they were still pink in the middle. Don't worry, you just browned the outside for flavor and next you'll thoroughly cook them in the marinara sauce. Also, cutting them at an angle instead of straight down provides more surface area in anticipation of soaking up all the heavenly flavors of the marinara, peppers, and onions.

cont.

SERVES 6

3 Tbsp olive oil

1 lb [455 g] sweet Italian sausage links

2 medium red bell peppers, cut into ¼ in [6 mm] thick strips

½ white onion, thinly sliced

1 garlic clove, minced

Kosher salt

Freshly ground black pepper

2 fresh basil leaves, torn

4 cups [960 ml] Simple Marinara (page 106)

6 sesame seed rolls, store-bought from your favorite bakery

6 thick slices aged provolone cheese

Transfer the sausage pieces back to the pot with the peppers and onions, add the basil and marinara, and cook uncovered, stirring now and then, until everyone in the pot becomes good, good friends and their flavors meld and your whole house fills with the fragrance of softened sweet peppers and porky sausage, about 45 minutes.

Remove from the heat and allow to cool slightly before (stabbing a hunk with your fork and eating it on the sly?—I do it, too!) dividing the sausage and pepper mixture among the sesame seed rolls and topping each with a thick slice of aged provolone. Put on the Eagles game and serve immediately.

BURGER CRAVE Satisfying a craving for a Little Owl Bacon Cheeseburger at home is really easy. In fact, when you cook a burger on the stove top in a large, shallow frying pan, in a cast-iron skillet, or on a flat griddle, you can achieve complete caramelization on the meat, since the entire surface area of the burger is in contact with your pan, which means a lot of flavor! Just resist the urge to squash down your burger in the skillet, since doing so will release all the treasured burger juices—unless, of course, you want a smash burger, which is another type of burger entirely (it's always made on a griddle). My burger blend and my cooking method let you have it both ways: knock-your-socks-off depth-of-flavor caramelization on the outside and a juicy middle that drips with flavor on the inside. Also, when cooking a burger indoors, you can maintain a consistent, even temperature on your stove top. But because I want you to shine like a star at summer cookouts, too, if you choose to cook my burger on your outdoor grill over an open flame, here's a tip: Keep a spray bottle of water close at hand and douse any large flame flare-up that may happen when the fat falls on the coals. You need to manage the temperature between ember and flame versus fat. You don't want the flame licking at the meat, or your burger will take on the unpleasant taste of the flame oil. Controlling those embers so that they burn at a moderate heat is the best way to achieve a smoky flavor and optimal caramelization, which will thrill you. I'm thrilled just talking about it!

LITTLE OWL BACON CHEESEBURGER

My Little Owl burger is a proprietary blend of meat made from fresh sirloin, short rib, and brisket from Manhattan's legendary meat purveyor Pat LaFreida. If you want to order a custom burger blend directly from LaFreida meats, go for it! They ship all over the country. The secret to making a thrilling burger—one in which you get the caramelized outside and the juicy inside—begins with selecting the meats that will give you the most marbled fat, so that when the fat melts it keeps the burger juicy. Ask your butcher to make a custom blend comprised of chuck, round, and brisket cuts with a 70/30 lean-to-fat ratio. And when you use the Harrison spice mixture, you'll set this burger apart from your neighbor down the block. (It's not a contest, but it doesn't hurt to get a great burger reputation!) The spice adds funk and heat from the Madras curry, and when it mingles with the juices from the melted fat of the burger, it creates that Little Owl signature flavor in the caramelized crusty outside. And here's a tip: Tuck the bacon under the cheese so it doesn't slip 'n' slide.

cont.

SERVES 6

12 slices thick-cut bacon, preferably applewood-smoked

3 lb [1.4 kg] burger blend (see headnote)

1 tsp kosher salt

Freshly ground black pepper

The Harrison Spice Mix (page 18)

6 slices good-quality aged Cheddar cheese

6 sesame seed burger buns

cont.

Preheat a large nonstick griddle or heavy skillet over medium-high heat for 5 minutes. Place your bacon slices on the hot griddle and cook until the fat renders and they crisp, about 1 minute. Set aside.

Place the burger blend in a large bowl and add the salt and several grinds of pepper to the meat. Using your clean hands, mix well to combine.

Divide the meat equally into six 8 oz [230 g] balls (you can use your hands to separate the meat mixture, right in the bowl, or measure them out), then flatten each ball into a patty about ¾ in [2 cm] thick. Sprinkle both sides of each patty with pinches of the Harrison spice mixture.

Place the burgers on the griddle or skillet over medium-high heat and cook until the underside of the burger gets nicely browned and the fat melts, about 3 minutes. Flip and cook on the other side, about 3 minutes more for medium-rare or 4 minutes for medium. Don't be tempted to squash the burger down or flatten it with a spatula (see "Burger Crave," page 51). Just let it do its thing and flip it only once. Top each burger with 2 slices of bacon and 1 slice of cheese during the last minute of cooking.

Place a burger on the bottom half of each bun, top with the remaining bun halves, and transfer to a serving platter, alongside the lettuce, tomatoes, red onions, and your favorite pickles (I love Guss's half-sour pickles) and condiments. Serve immediately.

½ head iceberg lettuce, roughly torn

1 beefsteak tomato, thinly sliced

1 red onion, ends trimmed, peeled, and thinly sliced

6 half-sour pickles

CHAPTER

2

Soups and Salads

❧ Soups and Salads

At Little Owl, my staff knows that when we sit down to eat together, I'm the one who always finishes the family meal salad, usually asking rhetorically, "You guys mind if I kill that?" Growing up, a Sunday supper wasn't complete without one of my mom-mom's iceberg lettuce *salits* (it's how we pronounced "salad") on the table. And many of these soups and salad recipes are dishes I crave and love to cook at home. Several of them are intimately connected to my childhood memories: what my mom would make when we had a nasty cold, my mom-mom's use of escarole in soup, the celebration of summer's arrival with roadside corn stands dotting our drive down the Jersey Shore with my dad. And the time I fell in love at The Pub (see page 74). And many of these dishes, such as my Onion Soup Gratin (page 61), taste just as amazing at home as they do on a snowy day at Little Owl. Because I want to show you how to do it right!

A few words on soup making: There is a kind of slow-down, good-cooking vibe that comes from chopping vegetables. For you, cutting vegetables to make soup might be a big pain and you're tempted to take out the chopper. Just don't. There are plenty of times to use valuable shortcuts in life (and cooking) and times to take it slow and just enjoy the journey getting there. I can think of dozens of things in the kitchen that require slowing down so that your focus and patience build your kitchen confidence: learning to feel your way through making fresh pasta so that you know just how much flour to add; letting onions cook slowly and not being afraid that they are burning when their sugars release and they turn black and your pan looks like hell; stirring the Sunday gravy; and, of course, chopping carrots, celery, and onions (the list goes on and on). So please, when there are specific directions in *any* recipe to chop vegetables by hand and you wonder why you can't just use your Cuisinart, rest assured that it's because the final outcome of a dish determines the approach to preparing and cooking it. Think of these soup and salad recipes and cooking techniques as opportunities to earn your confidence and build trust in your kitchen so that you can cook from a place of joy, comfort, and consistency.

Ribollita *("The Flu Shot")* **59**

Onion Soup Gratin **61**

Summer Corn Chowder *with Lobster* **64**

Italian Wedding Soup
with Mini Meatballs and Egg Drop **67**

Sherry Shallot Vinaigrette **69**

Citrus and Palm Hearts Salad **70**

Spinach, Avocado, and
Strawberries *with Lemon Poppyseed Dressing* **73**

Sunflower Salad *with Golden Beets* **74**

Little Gem Caesar *with Panko Crunchies* **78**

Warm Radicchio, Pancetta,
and Gorgonzola **79**

RIBOLLITA
("The Flu Shot")

At the first sign of a runny nose, my mom would put this soup on the stove, dubbing it "the flu shot." Incredibly delicious, nutritious, and simple to make—you toss all the ingredients into one pot and bring them to a boil—it's inspired by the Tuscan winter classic *ribollita*, meaning "re-boiled." You will want to make this soup 1 day in advance so that you give it time to cool overnight in your refrigerator. This is when the magic happens and the flavors meld with the bread and the beans. My version starts with a nutritious Homemade Chicken Broth (page 148), but a store-bought broth is perfectly acceptable. Also, you can get creative with the vegetables you want to add. I prefer Tuscan black kale—look for lacinato or dinosaur kale at the farmers' market or grocery store—but you can dream up a ribollita with Swiss chard, mustard greens, or collard greens. And if you have a potato lying around or any other scrap vegetables, feel free to add them to the pot. Use this recipe as your guide to goodness. But one point I am going to be firm with you on is this: Don't even think about using a microwave to reheat this soup. That is not big love—that's negligence. And it won't taste the same. We understand each other, though, so I am not worried.

Preheat the oven to 400°F [200°C]. Line a baking sheet with parchment paper.

Place the bread pieces on the prepared baking sheet and toast until brown and crusty, about 4 minutes. Set aside.

Meanwhile, prepare an herb bouquet by gathering the thyme, rosemary, and bay leaves into a bundle and tying them together using unwaxed kitchen string. Set aside.

In a large cast-iron Dutch oven or pot over medium heat, warm the olive oil. Add the garlic and cook for 30 seconds. Add the chicken broth, herb bouquet, kale, carrots, celery and celery leaves, onion, beans, and toasted bread. Bring to a boil, then lower the heat to a simmer and cook, uncovered, for 1 hour.

cont.

SERVES 4

4 oz [115 g] crusty Italian bread, torn into bite-size pieces (I like pane pugliese)

3 fresh thyme sprigs

1 fresh rosemary sprig

3 fresh bay leaves

¼ cup [60 ml] olive oil

3 large garlic cloves, minced

8 cups [2 L] chicken broth, homemade or store-bought

6 oz [170 g] fresh kale, stems removed and leaves roughly cut into ½ in [12 mm] strips

3 medium carrots, peeled and cut into ½ in [12 mm] dice

3 stalks celery, cut into ½ in [12 mm] dice, plus the leaves

1 medium white onion, ends trimmed, unpeeled, and cut into ½ in [12 mm] dice

One 15 oz [425 g] can cannellini beans, drained and rinsed

Maldon sea salt

½ cup [50 g] finely grated fresh Parmesan cheese, for serving

An excellent extra-virgin olive oil, for serving

Freshly ground black pepper

Using tongs, fish out the herb bouquet and discard. Turn off the heat and let the soup cool for 30 minutes before covering with a lid and refrigerating overnight. The next day is "re-bollita" time! When ready to serve, return the pot to the stove, uncover, and slowly bring the soup to life by bringing to a boil over low heat, boiling for 5 minutes.

Divide the soup among four deep soup bowls. Sprinkle each serving with a pinch of Maldon sea salt flakes, Parmesan cheese, a drizzle of extra-virgin olive oil, and a few grinds of pepper. Serve immediately. Store leftovers in an airtight container in your refrigerator for up to 4 days.

THE UGLY PART Here is the ugly part that I want you to embrace that not a lot of recipes tell you about onion soup. At some point in this 1½-hour-long (give or take a few minutes) caramelization process, the bottom of your pot will begin to turn filthy and black in spots. That is the natural sugar being released from the onions, blackening, and sticking. Do not be alarmed. It is our friend. I used to have to hide the onion pot at another restaurant I worked at so no one would take it away and clean it and toss what looked to be black and dirty onions. Your onions are not burnt, unless you really did burn them. And, in that case, you'll smell it. So, ask yourself if you cut them too thin, raised the heat too high when I told you low, or walked away and forgot about them completely. If you did, toss them out and start over. Sometimes, the very best things we learn when cooking are the things we are told *not* to do. In this case, do not pull those onions off the heat until the bottom of the pot is sufficiently blackened, and your onions are lovingly and slowly browned.

ONION SOUP GRATIN

I want you to master making this onion soup by teaching you how to fear-lessly embrace caramelizing onions. Caramelizing is a slow-cooking process that allows the natural sugars in the onions to release and then incorporate into the broth to create the deep, rich, sweet onion soup flavor that you long for on a wintry day. Sounds romantic? No. It gets ugly. But good-ugly (see "The Ugly Part," above). Making this soup takes a few professional chef moves along with a good dose of mom-mom patience. I'm here for you.

But before we begin, a word about the broth: I use a chicken broth base plus veal demi-glace (a classic French brown sauce made from veal bones that gives the broth a dark, meaty flavor). The act of making veal demi-glace is like staying up all night long for a friend who needs you. Literally. Because this stuff cooks all night. And since I love you too much to hand you such a time-consuming task when all you want is a fantastic-tasting bowl of onion soup, I will tell you that store-bought demi-glace (look for D'Artagnan) makes an excellent substitute. However, should you opt to use a homemade or store-bought beef stock, eliminate the veal demi-glace. OK, here we go.

cont.

SERVES 4

Caramelized Onions

¼ cup [60 ml] extra-virgin olive oil, plus more for drizzling

4 lb [1.8 kg] Spanish onions, ends trimmed, peeled, and cut into ¼ in [6 mm] thick slices

¼ cup [60 g] kosher salt

Soup

4 cups [960 ml] chicken broth, homemade (page 148) or store-bought

½ cup [120 ml] Spanish sherry

½ cup [120 ml] store-bought veal demi-glace

1 tsp sambal chili paste

cont.

Gratin

¼ cup [20 g] grated
fontina cheese

¼ cup [25 g] grated
Gruyère cheese

¼ cup [15 g] finely
grated pecorino cheese

¼ cup [25 g] finely grated
fresh Parmesan cheese

1 crusty baguette, cut
into eight ¼ in
[6 mm] thick slices

Freshly ground
black pepper

Snipped fresh chives,
for garnish

To make the caramelized onions: In a large cast-iron Dutch oven or a large shallow pot with a lot of surface area, warm the olive oil over low heat. Place the sliced onions in the pot and use a wooden spoon to separate them, breaking up the rings and spreading them out into a uniform layer. Do not let them clump in a pile at any point throughout cooking. Sprinkle them with the kosher salt and cook until the onions are very soft and brown and black spots appear on the bottom of your pot, about 1½ hours (see "The Ugly Part," page 61). Every 10 minutes or so, use a wooden spoon to stir and re-spread them on the bottom of the pot.

This step isn't absolutely necessary, but you should know it for caramelizing onions for other dishes. Once you are confident that you have achieved the level of ugly necessary to proceed, remove the pot from the heat and let rest for about 10 minutes.

Using a rubber spatula (or the back of a wooden spoon) and applying gentle pressure, gently swirl the onions around and watch the sticky, black sugar melt. Incorporate the sugars right into the onions by continuing to gently scrape the bottom of the pot and folding the loosened sugars into the onions until the bottom of the pot is clean and the color of your onions is dark brownish black. Now taste it. It should have a sweet, deep, rich onion flavor.

To make the soup: Return your pot to the stove over medium-high heat, and add the chicken broth, sherry, veal demi-glace, and chili paste. Bring to a boil and then lower the heat and simmer for 20 minutes.

Meanwhile, preheat the oven to 400°F [200°C]. Line a baking sheet with aluminum foil.

To make the gratin: In a large bowl, add the fontina, Gruyère, pecorino, and Parmesan and mix well to incorporate. Set aside. Place the baguette slices in a single layer on the prepared baking sheet and drizzle each one with olive oil. Toast until crispy, about 10 minutes. Top each slice with a mound of mixed cheeses, dividing the cheese evenly until you've used it up. Return the cheese-covered toast to the oven and toast until the cheese is bubbly and browned, 5 minutes.

Divide the onion soup among four deep bowls and top each with two cheese croutons, a few cracks of pepper, and snipped chives. Serve immediately.

6 fresh thyme sprigs

1 fresh bay leaf

1 lb [455 g] asparagus, ends
trimmed and discarded

6 ears corn, in the husk

1 Tbsp kosher salt

1 large Spanish onion,
ends trimmed, peeled,
and thinly sliced

4 garlic cloves, halved

One 2 lb [910 g] lobster,
alive and pinching

½ cup [120 ml] Chablis or
other crisp, dry white wine

2 Tbsp unsalted butter

2 medium carrots, peeled
and roughly chopped

3 stalks celery,
roughly chopped

1 medium white onion,
ends trimmed, peeled,
and roughly chopped

½ cup [120 ml] heavy cream

Extra-virgin olive oil,
for drizzling

Snipped fresh chives,
for garnish

SUMMER CORN CHOWDER
with Lobster

I love coming across big, gnarly piles of stacked, unhusked corn at my local farmers' market or a roadside stand. In my part of the world, I cook with Jersey corn—it's sweeter and tastes better than New York corn in my opinion, and it grows bigger, too! But you can use any sweet summer corn at the peak of flavor; just stay away from prepackaged, husked ears wrapped in plastic. Look for rough-hewn bunches. Many classic corn chowder recipes call for boiling or soaking your corn, but when you simplify it and just lay your unhusked ears out on a baking tray, the corn steams inside the husk, cooking evenly without any extra mess (always a good thing!). The addition of the entire lobster, right into the broth, allows the fat and shells to impart a deep ocean sweetness throughout the chowder. And a little bit of cream goes a long way to lend a silky smoothness that doesn't mask the pure corn flavor.

Preheat the oven to 375°F [190°C].

Prepare an herb bouquet by gathering the thyme and bay leaf into a bundle and tying them together using unwaxed kitchen string. Set aside. Prepare an ice water bath by filling a large bowl (preferably metal) with cold water and ice cubes. Set aside.

Meanwhile, bring a large pot of generously salted water to a boil. Add the asparagus and boil until the spears turn a bright green color and are tender, 3 to 4 minutes. Using tongs, pull out the asparagus, plunge them into the ice water, and let cool for about 1 minute. Remove and cut into 1 in [2.5 cm] pieces and set aside.

Lay the whole ears of corn on a baking sheet and roast in the oven for 45 minutes.

Remove and set aside to cool. When the corn is cool enough to handle, remove the silks and husks. Working with one ear of corn at a time, stand it up, tip down on a cutting board. Using a sharp knife, carefully remove the kernels by slicing downward along the ear. Since the corn is cooked, they should slice off easily and not fling around too much. Transfer to a bowl and set aside.

Cut the corncobs in half, place them in a large pot, and add 6 cups [1.4 L] of water. Add the salt, Spanish onion, garlic, and herb bouquet. Set the pot over high heat and bring to a gentle rolling boil—you'll know it's a rolling boil when you can't get in the pot to stir it because it's moving so fast. But you don't want it so agitated that it makes a mess and bubbles over. Maintain a gentle rolling boil for about 20 minutes.

Meanwhile, we have to kill that lobster. Place the lobster on a cutting board, belly down, and using a sharp knife, plunge it between the lobster's eyes. Now it is dead. In order for the entire lobster to fit in the pot, you have to break it into pieces. The preferred method is to break the lobster apart with your hands by holding it at the head and twisting and pulling off the tail. Repeat with the claws; twist and pull. (Once removed, snip off those rubber bands that hold them together.) Completely split the head off the body to expose the innards and, piece by piece, add the lobster to the pot, along with the wine and 1 cup [240 ml] of water, using tongs to move aside the corn cobs and making sure that the lobster pieces are submerged.

Return the pot to a boil and cook until the lobster shells turn bright red, about 10 minutes.

Remove from the heat and, using tongs, remove the lobster pieces and set aside to cool. Use a colander set over a large heat-proof bowl and strain the liquid, pressing the solids against the bottom with a wooden spoon, squeezing out every bit of flavor. Reserve the liquid for your corn stock. Discard the rest.

In the same, now-empty pot, melt the butter over medium heat. Add the carrots, celery, white onion, and half of the reserved corn kernels. Cook, stirring continuously, until the carrots and celery soften and the onion is translucent, 6 to 7 minutes.

Add the reserved corn stock, raise the heat to high, and bring it to a gentle rolling boil for about 15 minutes. Remove the soup from the heat, transfer to a blender, and add the heavy cream. Purée the soup to a smooth consistency, about 30 seconds.

Set a fine-mesh sieve over a large, clean pot and strain the puréed chowder to achieve a velvety texture, removing any little lumps as you swirl it with the back of a wooden spoon through the sieve. Set aside.

Meanwhile, crack the lobster pieces, removing the meat from the tail and the claws. Chop the meat into medium pieces and add them to the chowder along with the reserved asparagus and the remaining corn kernels. Turn the heat to medium and simmer until warmed through, 1 to 2 minutes.

To serve, divide the soup among six bowls and top with drizzles of extra-virgin olive oil and some snipped chives.

HOW TO GIVE YOUR "SCHKA-ROLE" A BATH (LIKE A MOM-MOM) To get dirty escarole clean, give it an old-school tub bath in your sink. Fill your clean sink with very cold water and dunk your escarole up and down. Drain the sink (you'll see a ton of dirt left behind) and rinse away the dirt at the bottom. Roughly chop the escarole. Fill your clean sink back up with cold water, toss in the chopped escarole, dunk it under, watch it float to the top, use your hands to remove it, and set it aside in a big bowl. Drain the sink, rinse the dirt, and repeat, filling the sink and dunking the escarole for a third time. The last time that you remove the escarole, place it in your salad spinner. Gently spin the escarole a few times to remove excess water. By the way, do not pound that little brake on the top—I know you do it 'cause it's fun; I've seen you. But it kills delicate lettuces, so control the speed! Now your escarole is fresh, clean, and ready.

ITALIAN WEDDING SOUP
with Mini Meatballs and Egg Drop

Although I've seen this soup served at plenty of Italian-American weddings that I've been to, Italian wedding soup gets its name from the happy marriage of flavors that come together with the meatballs, vegetables, and chicken broth. It was known in my house as "*schka-role*" soup for the escarole greens that float in the broth. To get it good and clean, see "How to Give Your 'Schka-role' a Bath," above. This soup is not only a Little Owl favorite, but also one of my favorite soups to make on a day off. While Italian wedding soup doesn't always have an egg in it, I love adding one—it's inspired by the classic Italian stracciatella soup *and* my love of Chinese egg drop soup! My grandmother's moist and tender meatballs are rolled into a mini version so that you can fit them on your spoon in one bite. And baking them in the oven before dropping them in the soup firms them up so that they don't turn to mush. Here's a science fact from a grand-mom chef: If you bake the meatballs ahead of time and hold them in the refrigerator or freezer in an airtight container until ready to make the soup, the natural gelatin that forms from the combo of fat, protein, and water in the meatball mix will release in the hot broth, ensuring that they will be oh-so-juicy.

Preheat the oven to 350°F [180°C]. Drizzle a baking sheet with olive oil and set aside.

cont.

SERVES 4

Meatballs

5¼ oz [150 g] ground beef

5¼ oz [150 g] ground pork

5¼ oz [150 g] ground veal

2 eggs

½ cup [30 g] panko bread crumbs

¼ cup [15 g] finely grated pecorino cheese

½ tsp kosher salt

¼ tsp freshly ground black pepper

¼ cup [10 g] finely chopped fresh Italian parsley leaves

cont.

Soup

2 Tbsp neutral oil, such as canola

3 medium carrots, peeled and cut into ½ in [12 mm] dice

3 stalks celery, cut into ½ in [12 mm] dice, plus the leaves

1 medium white onion, ends trimmed, unpeeled, and cut into ½ in [12 mm] dice

1 garlic clove, minced

1 lb [455 g] escarole, bathed, tough outer leaves and roots removed, and roughly chopped (see "How to Give Your 'Schka-Role' a Bath," page 67)

6 cups [1.4 L] chicken broth, homemade (page 148) or store-bought

4 eggs

½ cup [50 g] finely grated pecorino cheese, for finishing

An excellent extra-virgin olive oil, for finishing

Freshly ground black pepper

To make the meatballs: In a large bowl, combine the beef, pork, veal, eggs, ⅓ cup [80 ml] of cold water, bread crumbs, cheese, salt, pepper, and parsley. Use your hands to mix well and form tightly into 20 bite-size mini meatballs, about 1 oz [28 g] each. Transfer the meatballs to the baking sheet and bake until the meatballs are brown and firm, about 15 minutes.

Meanwhile, to make the soup: In a large pot over medium-high heat, warm the neutral oil until it shimmers. Add the carrots, celery and celery leaves, onion, and garlic and cook, stirring, until the vegetables are soft, 3 to 5 minutes. Cooking them in the oil first ensures that their aromatics get released and flavors your soup. Add the chopped escarole and chicken broth. Using a wooden spoon, stir everything together, turn the heat to high, and bring to a boil. Lower the heat to a simmer, add the baked mini meatballs, and cook, stirring every so often, for about 30 minutes.

Just before serving, crack the eggs into a small bowl, use a fork to whisk, then slowly drizzle into the simmering soup. Watch the egg cook from the heat (move it around with your wooden spoon) and disperse into floating eggy bundles.

Divide the soup among four bowls (two meatballs for you/two meatballs for me, etc.) and finish with generous sprinkles of pecorino, a drizzle of extra-virgin olive oil, and black pepper. Reserve any leftovers in an airtight container and store for up to 4 days in your refrigerator.

MY MOTHER SAUCE In the early days of my career while working at Symphony Café in New York City, I was promoted to one of the most esteemed positions in a professional kitchen: saucier, a.k.a. "the guy who makes all the sauces." It's an important gig, especially in a French kitchen, because sauces go with everything. And I credit my stint as a saucier with helping shape my kitchen confidence. Established more than one hundred years ago, the five classic mother sauces are velouté, espagnole, sauce tomat, béchamel, and hollandaise. And with the addition of meat, herbs, spices, or vegetables, they can be spun into so many offspring!

SHERRY SHALLOT VINAIGRETTE

While I am as old-school as they come, I do take a modern approach to including mayonnaise and vinaigrette on my list of mother sauces. Think about it: You can transform a basic homemade or store-bought mayonnaise with herbs or pesto and you can cook with it (Halibut with Basil Pesto, Sweet Corn, and Pea Salad, page 177). It's totally legit! This Sherry Shallot Vinaigrette is the base from which all of my dressings start; you can add anchovies to it (Grilled Scallops with Chicories, Bread Crumbs, and Anchovy Dressing, page 175); combine it with cranberry sauce (Thanksgiving Bibb and Beets, page 77), lemon and poppyseeds (Spinach, Avocado, and Strawberries with Lemon Poppyseed Dressing, page 73), or truffle oil (Long Island Duck Breast with Cherries and Arugula, page 153); and even use it as a marinade to cook with (Salad Dressing Chicken with Escarole and White Beans, page 142). With space so limited at Little Owl and at home, creating Sherry Shallot Vinaigrette is my finest example of necessity being the mother (sauce) of invention. I hope you love it as much as I do! Note: See the subrecipes for a handy reference for smaller batch versions—I did the work for you, because we're good friends.

In a small bowl, combine the vinegar, honey, mustard, and shallot and whisk to blend. Slowly add the oil and whisk until combined. Transfer to an airtight container and refrigerate indefinitely until ready to use. Once opened, it will keep for up to 2 weeks.

¾ CUP [180 ML]

¼ cup [60 ml] sherry vinegar

2 Tbsp honey

1 Tbsp Dijon mustard

1 shallot, finely diced

½ cup [120 ml] extra-virgin olive oil

½ CUP [120 ML]

¼ cup [60 ml] sherry vinegar

2 tsp honey

2 tsp Dijon mustard

1 shallot, finely diced

¼ [60 ml] cup extra-virgin olive oil

¼ CUP [60 ML]

2 Tbsp sherry vinegar

1 tsp honey

1 tsp Dijon mustard

1 small shallot, finely diced

¼ cup [60 ml] extra-virgin olive oil

SERVES 4

1 medium Ruby
Red grapefruit

1 medium orange
(navel, blood, Cara Cara
varieties are all great!)

10 Castelvetrano
olives, pitted and
roughly chopped

4 fresh basil leaves, torn

2 cups [40 g] packed
arugula leaves

1 small Belgian endive or
1 small head radicchio,
outer leaves discarded,
halved and thinly sliced
lengthwise

One 14 oz [400 g]
can hearts of palm,
drained, rinsed, and
thinly sliced lengthwise

Maldon sea salt

Freshly ground
black pepper

¼ cup [60 ml] Sherry
Shallot Vinaigrette
(page 69)

CITRUS AND PALM HEARTS SALAD

This classic winter Sicilian salad includes my favorite vibrant green Castelvetrano Sicilian olives. They are meaty and buttery on the palate and a touch sweet. To remove the pits, gently tap them with the flat side of your meat mallet. If you want to swap out another green olive, look for smaller, fruitier Taggiasca olives from the coastal region of Liguria. Ligurian olive oil, made from Taggiasca olives, is a rich oil fantastic for finishing or slathering on warm bread. Hearts of palm, which look like white asparagus and taste similar to an artichoke, are sold in a can and are a versatile addition to give this salad some crunch. You can use any combination of citrus fruits for a burst of sunshine. Cutting the citrus into supremes—segments with the bitter pith and tough membrane removed— makes them look beautiful in the salad and allows their juices to mingle with the dressing.

Using a very sharp paring knife, cut off the ends of the grapefruit. Place a flat side on a cutting board and, starting from the top and following the natural shape of the fruit, cut off the peel and the pith. Work your way around the grapefruit until you're left with a bald fruit ball. The easiest way to proceed with maximum control and ease is to cup the fruit ball on its side in your hand, and then gently remove the segments by slicing along the adjacent membranes (the white part that holds the segments together) toward the center of the fruit until the cuts meet. As you release a segment, transfer it to a large mixing bowl. Gently rotate the ball in your hand and repeat, working your way around the fruit until all the segments are released. Repeat the supreme maneuver with your orange, adding the segments to the same bowl.

To the grapefruit and orange segments, add the olives, basil, arugula, endive, hearts of palm, a pinch of salt flakes, and a few grinds of pepper. Pour the vinaigrette over the salad, tossing with your clean hands to coat everything.

Transfer the salad to a beautiful serving platter. Serve immediately.

SPINACH, AVOCADO, AND STRAWBERRIES
with Lemon Poppyseed Dressing

SERVES 4

½ cup [120 ml] Sherry Shallot Vinaigrette (page 69)

2 Tbsp fresh lemon juice

2 tsp poppyseeds

6 oz [170 g] fresh strawberries, stemmed, hulled, and sliced

2 cups [40 g] arugula

2 cups [40 g] packed spinach leaves, washed, dried, and roughly torn

1 large avocado, diced

Maldon sea salt

Freshly ground black pepper

I made my first poppyseed dressing when I was working with Chef Andrew Humbert, a former executive chef for the legendary Louisiana chef Paul Prudhomme, who brought Louisiana Creole cooking to the mainstream. Creamy and sweet salad dressings are popular in the South, but when I first encountered them I didn't think they made much sense! This South Philly kid was accustomed to the bright acidity of my mom-mom's Old-School "Salit" (page 237). But the flavor is undeniably delicious. Achieving a creamy dressing is fast and easy when you use your blender, as the mustard in the base of the dressing emulsifies. Andrew Humbert also helped build my kitchen confidence by illuminating the fact that if I could build amazing flavor in Sunday Gravy (page 211), I would be a natural at one-pot gumbo! (I love to cook it with my buddy and New Orleans native August Goulet, who is an expert!) And the colors in this salad? Green avocado, white poppyseed dressing, and red strawberries: a nod to both the Italian flag and the other boot, too—Louisiana!

In a blender, combine the vinaigrette and lemon juice. Blend until creamy, about 30 seconds. Stir in the poppyseeds and set aside.

In a large bowl, combine the strawberries, arugula, spinach, and avocado. Pour the dressing over everything and add a pinch of salt flakes and a few grinds of pepper. Using your hands (or tongs), gently toss to coat the salad, being careful not to mush up the avocado too much. Transfer to a serving platter and serve immediately. (So pretty!)

I FELL IN LOVE AT THE PUB If we were on our best behavior, my father would take us to The Pub as a treat. It is a family steakhouse restaurant in New Jersey with a dining room that's set up to look like a medieval castle with huge beams and vaulted ceilings. Every kid's dream! It still has wood-burning ovens and round tables like King Arthur's castle. As a kid, I was always so impressed that they gave you a knife with your bread. And if we were lucky, we'd get a few quarters to play the video games in the lobby! My cousin Thomas and I would steal cigarette butts that had been extinguished prematurely out of the sand-filled ashtrays in the bathroom while our fathers would get drunk at the bar. Come to think of it, they would always seat my family in the back corner, far, far away from everyone else. But, apart from the décor, delicious food, and fun, The Pub was, in my eyes, so special because they had a salad bar. And it was at *that* salad bar that I fell in love with sunflower seeds on a salad. That concept blew my mind! There they were, already shelled and toasted just waiting for me. Fast-forward to 2001 to the opening of The Harrison in Tribeca; Jimmy Bradley and I developed a version of this salad with sunflower seeds, paying tribute to my Pub salad bar fascination. Jimmy's sunflower salad is a lot fancier than my version (his version is in his book, *The Red Cat Cookbook*), but I knew when I opened Little Owl that I had to reinvent it as my own. If you are ever passing through Pennsauken, New Jersey, I implore you to stop in at The Pub and make your own memories.

SERVES 4

4 small golden beets, skins on, unwashed (any leafy green tops trimmed and reserved for cooking like escarole if you like)

1 Tbsp unsalted butter

1 Tbsp olive oil

½ cup [70 g] sunflower seeds

Maldon sea salt

1 head Boston Bibb lettuce, roughly torn

Large handful frisée lettuce, torn into pieces

cont.

SUNFLOWER SALAD
with Golden Beets

My Bibb and beet salad has been on the menu at Little Owl since we opened in 2006, and its components turn with the seasons. I want you to have a salad that you love—one that you can riff on depending on the time of year. Since we opened in the spring, its original incarnation includes sunflower seeds, sprouts, and sunshine-colored golden beets, tossed with frisée and Bibb lettuces. In the fall and winter, I keep the base of the salad, but swap out sunflower seeds for pumpkin seeds and add blanched squash along with the beets. You can also create my holiday version for your Thanksgiving table with cranberry vinaigrette and turkey cracklings (see "Seasonal Spin-Offs," page 77). The texture of Bibb lettuce is both creamy and crunchy, delicate yet sturdy enough to hold up to the squash and the beets. And the outer leaves are great for lettuce wraps.

cont.

Large handful
sunflower sprouts

2 Tbsp roughly chopped
fresh Italian parsley

¼ cup [60 ml] Sherry
Shallot Vinaigrette
(page 69)

Freshly ground black
pepper

½ cup [50 g]
finely grated fresh
Parmesan cheese

Bring a large pot of generously salted water to a boil. Carefully place the beets in the water and boil for 8 minutes. Use a slotted spoon to remove them from the water and place them on a baking sheet to cool down a bit in your refrigerator.

Meanwhile, in a large pan over low heat, combine the butter and olive oil until melted. Add the sunflower seeds and toast them, alternating the heat of the pan from low to medium. My tip when toasting any seed or nut: Don't walk away from the pan. Stay in front of it and keep the seeds moving by shaking the pan back and forth, or they will burn! Toast until lightly golden in color, 2 to 3 minutes. Sprinkle with a pinch of salt and set aside.

Use a clean kitchen towel to hold a beet and gently apply pressure to the bottom, until it squeezes right out of its skin. So easy! Discard the skin. Repeat with the remaining beets. Quarter the beets with a sharp knife, transfer to a small bowl, and set aside.

Place the Bibb lettuce, frisée, sunflower sprouts, parsley, beets, and sunflower seeds in a large bowl and pour the vinaigrette over it. Add a generous pinch of Maldon sea salt and few grinds of pepper. Toss the salad around with your clean hands to coat everything. Finish with Parmesan cheese and set it on your table. Or divide among four plates and serve immediately.

SEASONAL SPIN-OFFS

Bibb and Beets with Pumpkin Seeds

When the weather gets cool and thoughts turn to pumpkins, eliminate the summery sunflower seeds and sprouts and add blanched squash and pumpkin seeds to the Bibb lettuce, golden beets, and frisée mix. Blanching simply means dipping a vegetable in boiling water, removing it, and cooling it down. Ice baths speed up the process, but whenever possible I recommend cooling in the refrigerator.

Prepare a 1 lb [455 g] butternut squash or delicata squash by peeling, halving, and removing the seeds. Cut into slices about 1 in [2.5 cm] thick.

Bring a large pot of water to a boil, and add the squash (you'll have to wait a few moments for the water to come back up to a boil). Once the water starts to boil again, using a slotted spoon, remove the squash and transfer to a baking sheet to cool in the refrigerator, about 20 minutes. Meanwhile, toast ½ cup [70 g] hulled pumpkin seeds. Once the squash has had time to cool, assemble the salad as you would the Sunflower Salad with Golden Beets (page 74).

Thanksgiving Bibb and Beets

In 2006, I appeared (full of hustle and heart) on *Food Network Challenge*'s "Ultimate Thanksgiving Feast" as one of my classic, scrappy South Philly moves in the hope of winning $10,000 in prize money so that I could open Little Owl. And holy turkey, I won! I made a holiday version of my Bibb and Beets with Pumpkin Seeds replete with a cranberry vinaigrette, turkey cracklings, and Madras curry–seasoned pumpkin seeds. To make my Thanksgiving version, prepare the Bibb and Beets with Pumpkin Seeds (above) with these additions and tweaks: For the pumpkin seeds, season them with a pinch of The Harrison Spice Mix (page 18) just before toasting. For the dressing, simply whisk ¼ cup [60 ml] of your own cranberry sauce into my Sherry Shallot Vinaigrette (page 69). Add 4 oz [115 g] trimmed, chopped, crispy turkey skin (cut it right off your bird and make it extra crispy by putting it in a hot skillet to render and crisp just like bacon). Add ¼ cup [35 g] dried cranberries for extra texture and cranberry zing.

Panko Crunchies

1 Tbsp unsalted butter

¼ cup [15 g] unseasoned panko bread crumbs

1 garlic clove, minced

1 Tbsp finely chopped fresh Italian parsley

Caesar

2 egg yolks (reserve the whites for an egg wash, omelet, or meringue)

¼ cup [25 g] finely grated fresh Parmesan cheese

4 fresh white Spanish boquerone anchovies (or in a pinch use 4 saltier, olive oil–packed anchovy fillets, drained)

2 Tbsp Dijon mustard

2 Tbsp red wine vinegar

Juice of ½ lemon

Dash of Worcestershire sauce

Dash of Tabasco sauce

1 tsp freshly ground black pepper

½ cup [60 ml] blended neutral oil, such as canola or vegetable

8 Little Gem lettuce hearts, leaves pulled apart

LITTLE GEM CAESAR
with Panko Crunchies

I made up Panko Crunchies—it's my name for toasted panko bread crumbs. It's just a simple way to give a quick and tasty, crumbly crouton feel to my salad by using a pantry staple. With small heads and sweet hearts, Little Gem is more often than not hydroponically grown and easy to find in your supermarket. Choose leaves that are approximately 2 to 3 in [5 to 7.5 cm] in length and bright green with a yellowish tone. Little Gem is a perfect vehicle for Caesar dressing because it looks and acts a lot like romaine, but its crispy, compact size means you can lay the whole heart on a plate and just drizzle the dressing over it—so easy! Also, this creamy dressing is stellar with escarole, kale, or bitter radicchio for an outside-the-box, easy Caesar salad anytime. The Dijon mustard is the hero (emulsifying agent) in this recipe, helping the oil and vinegar work it out so that they come together. And contrary to what your kitchen know-how wants to think about extra-virgin olive oil as the best to use in a salad dressing, when making my Caesar dressing, use a mild, neutral, blended oil to let the fresh, boquerone anchovy flavor shine.

To make the panko crunchies: In a large pan over medium-high heat, melt the butter, add the panko, and toast until the bread crumbs emit a pleasant nutty aroma and have an enticingly browned color, about 1 minute. Add the chopped garlic and toast for 45 seconds longer. Add the parsley, and using a wooden spoon, stir well to incorporate. Set aside.

To make the Caesar: In the work bowl of your food processor, add the egg yolks, Parmesan, anchovies, mustard, vinegar, lemon juice, Worcestershire, Tabasco, and black pepper. Pulse for a few seconds until smooth. With the processor running, slowly add the oil in a steady, refrained stream or it will cause the dressing to separate.

Divide the Little Gem lettuce hearts among four plates, spoon the dressing on top, and sprinkle with the Panko Crunchies. Serve immediately.

P.S. I love to serve this Little Gem Caesar alongside my Sangria-Marinated Skirt Steak (page 160) for an easy weeknight meal.

WARM RADICCHIO, PANCETTA, AND GORGONZOLA

In this Italian version of a blue cheese wedge salad, the pungent Gorgonzola, the fatty, salty warm pancetta, and the bitter radicchio get drizzled with a sweet balsamic reduction that you can also sprinkle over a soft cheese (I like La Tur from Piedmont) or some grilled peaches for dessert. It can keep in your refrigerator forever. Here, it adds a touch of sweetness to the bitter radicchio wedge. Someone asked me how I get the vegetables at Little Owl to taste so good. Apart from the fact that I let Mother Nature dictate what I make by cooking in season, when flavors are at their peak, I also try to satisfy all of our sweet, salty, bitter, and sour taste receptors in one bite! And this is one of those all-in-one-bite, happy-on-your-tongue dishes.

Preheat the oven to 400°F [200°C].

In a small saucepan over medium-high heat, add the balsamic and bring to a boil. Lower the heat and simmer until it reduces by half and gets syrupy enough to coat the back of a wooden spoon, about 7 minutes. Set aside.

Working with one radicchio wedge at a time, wrap each wedge with three raw pancetta slices. Place them on a baking sheet and roast until the pancetta is crispy, about 20 minutes.

Meanwhile, in a large bowl, combine the arugula, parsley, Gorgonzola, olive oil, and a few grinds of pepper. Using tongs, toss to combine. Divide the salad among four plates and place 1 or 2 of the radicchio wedges on top. Drizzle the balsamic reduction all over the radicchio wedges and serve immediately.

SERVES 4

1 cup [240 ml] balsamic vinegar

1 large head radicchio (about 8 oz [230 g]) or 2 small heads radicchio (about 6 oz [170 g] each), outer leaves discarded, root ends removed, and cut into 4 wedges each

8 oz [230 g] thinly sliced Italian pancetta

2 cups [40 g] arugula

¼ cup [10 g] roughly chopped fresh Italian parsley

½ cup [50 g] crumbled Gorgonzola cheese

2 Tbsp extra virgin olive oil

Freshly ground black pepper

CHAPTER

3

Vegetables

Vegetables

My menu decisions at Little Owl are determined by the seasons and what is available to me locally. And if you listen up, they talk to you! Simple summer Beefsteak Tomatoes (page 172) ask so little of me, just a few flakes of Maldon sea salt to enliven them. Because they are perfect. Because when we listen, the timing of Mother Nature is perfect. And connecting to her is important not just for our health, but also for the health of the planet. In the spring, mild, garlicky ramps grab hold of my senses. And what makes them such a treasure? They're gone so fast! The urgency I feel to scoop them up and pair them with everything becomes my spring obsession. New and tiny sweet peas carry me back to my father's favorite pea and ricotta–filled ravioli that we would eat around his birthday at Easter time. And Mexican-inspired summer corn swathed in mayonnaise is like shoveling summer right into my mouth. Delicata squash, Brussels sprouts, and escarole make me want to hunker down and welcome the cool breezes of fall. While many of my menu items at Little Owl, such as my Little Owl Crispy Chicken (page 146) and Little Owl Pork Chop with Parmesan Butter Beans (page 154), never change because they are my signature dishes, my best guideline for embracing seasonal cooking is through vegetables. And it was when I began to think this way that I started to become a better cook.

Pickled Red Onions 84

Pickled Fennel 85

Cucumber and Radish Pickles 86

Broccoli, Cauliflower, and Mushrooms *with Pepita Salsa Verde* 87

Roasted Corn, *Spicy Mexican Style* 89

Sesame Green Beans
with Mint, Chile, and Oyster Sauce **90**

Tender Broccoli Rabe
and Toasted Garlic **93**

Baked Eggplant Parmesan
with Soft Herb Salad **94**

Old-School Sweet Potatoes
and Ginger Ale **98**

Potato Fontina Fonduta 99

Curried Leek Home Fries 100

WATERCRESS SALAD AND PICKLED RED ONION

The acid from the pickles will mingle with the olive oil for a perfectly balanced, peppery, and lightly acidic watercress salad to serve alongside a rich meat dish.

SERVES 4

Several pickled red onions

3 oz [85 g] watercress, trimmed

2 to 3 Tbsp extra-virgin olive oil

Maldon sea salt, to taste

Freshly ground black pepper, to taste

In a large bowl, combine the ingredients. Use your hands to toss to combine and serve immediately.

MAKES 12 SERVINGS

2 cups [480 ml] rice wine vinegar

½ tsp red pepper flakes

1 medium red onion, ends trimmed, peeled, and sliced into thin rings

PICKLED LOVE A traditional pickle process starts with a very fresh vegetable or fruit, captured at its peak of flavor and then submerged in a hot brine that undergoes further hot water sterilization to inhibit bacterial growth. This is a beautiful, time-honored tradition and I love it, but I simply don't have the space to commit to it. So, here's a quick pickle that happens overnight in your refrigerator, to lend a bright acidity to red onions, fennel, cucumbers, and radishes. Since many of my dishes are bold and full of rich flavor, a little salad tossed with a bit of pickled vegetable goes a long way to balance that richness and complete the dish. Unlike a traditional process that preserves food for up to 1 year, these quick pickles are meant to last up to 1 month. Fast, spicy, and full of texture and flavor, they will make your family and friends say, "Wow! What's that refreshing-sour-spicy thing happening in my mouth?" Make these little pickles a top-secret ingredient in your cooking, without much fuss.

PICKLED RED ONIONS

Use these onions in a watercress salad (at left), serve them alongside my Lamb T-Bones (page 163), or sit them on top of Chicken Liver Mousse (page 140) toasts instead of pearl onions. Add them to sandwiches, tacos, or even on top of a Little Owl Bacon Cheeseburger (page 51) for a sublime burst of lightly pickled sweet onion.

In a large bowl, combine the vinegar and red pepper flakes. Submerge the onion slices in the mixture, placing a small plate on top to hold them down. Transfer to your refrigerator to chill overnight. The onions will turn a very pretty jewel tone, as will the vinegar. Once you use up your onions, keep the rose-colored vinegar to use in salad dressings. Transfer the entire contents to a glass jar (so you can see that pop of color each time you open the door) and store in your refrigerator for up to 1 month.

PICKLED FENNEL

This pickled fennel gets tossed with wild dandelion greens to create a beautiful flavor burst of texture on top of my Little Owl Pork Chop (page 154), enhancing the fennel seed in the pork marinade. Quick pickled fennel is also a terrific addition to tacos, on hot dogs (I love hot dogs!), or alongside a selection of your favorite cheeses with drizzles of olive oil and freshly ground black pepper.

MAKES 12 SERVINGS

2 cups [480 ml]
rice wine vinegar

½ tsp red pepper flakes

½ fennel bulb,
outer layers removed,
tough end trimmed

In a large bowl, combine the vinegar and red pepper flakes. Using a mandoline, lay the fennel, cut-side down, against the blade and thinly slice—little pieces may break away as you shave it; that's great—save them and toss them in, too. Submerge the fennel slices in the vinegar mixture, placing a small plate on top to hold them down. Transfer to your refrigerator to chill overnight. Transfer the entire contents to a glass jar and store in your refrigerator for up to 1 month.

3 Kirby cucumbers, cut into ½ in [12 mm] coins

6 breakfast radishes, trimmed and halved lengthwise

2 cups [480 ml] seasoned rice wine vinegar

¼ cup [50 g] sugar

2 Tbsp coarse salt

2 Tbsp sambal chili paste

1 Tbsp whole coriander seeds

Several fresh cilantro leaves, for serving

Freshly ground black pepper

Extra-virgin olive oil, for serving

CUCUMBER AND RADISH PICKLES

Have you ever bought seasoned rice wine vinegar by mistake and wondered what you can do with it? Me, too! It's too sweet for vinaigrette, but it's perfect for this quick, hot brine preparation for cucumbers and radishes. These are a refreshing and slightly crunchy addition to your picnic table and will last up to 1 month in the refrigerator.

Place the cucumbers and radishes in a large, heat-proof container and set aside.

In a large saucepan over medium-high heat, combine 2 cups [480 ml] of water, the vinegar, sugar, salt, chili paste, and coriander seeds, stirring to dissolve the sugar. Bring to a boil, then remove from the heat and pour the hot liquid over the cucumbers and radishes, placing a small plate on top to completely submerge them. Transfer to your refrigerator to chill overnight. Transfer the entire contents to a glass jar and store in your refrigerator for up to 1 month.

Drain each portion before serving and toss with fresh cilantro leaves, a crack of fresh pepper, and a drizzle of olive oil.

BROCCOLI, CAULIFLOWER, AND MUSHROOMS
with Pepita Salsa Verde

Most Italian *salsa verde* preparations include salty anchovies and the addition of a piquant component like capers or cornichons. Instead, I go for more of a pesto feel in my salsa verde, using *pepitas* (the Spanish word for pumpkin seeds), and serve this at Little Owl every fall, when that delightful pumpkin-picking feeling is in the air. The result is an herbaceous and intense pumpkin seed oil dressing. It's delicious when strewn across these roasted vegetables, but you can also use it as an accompaniment to other favorite dishes, like skirt steak or scrambled eggs. Note: Be sure to cut your cauliflower florets smaller than your broccoli florets, since cauliflower takes longer to cook.

Preheat the oven to 450°F [230°C]. Line a small baking sheet with paper towels. Line a large baking sheet with parchment paper.

To prepare the salsa verde: In a large skillet over high heat, warm the olive oil until it shimmers, add the pepitas, lower the heat to medium, and toast, stirring constantly with a wooden spoon until the seeds begin to turn toasty brown (they will also puff or even pop), 4 to 5 minutes. Continue to cook for 1 minute more, add the salt, give it a stir, then remove ¼ cup [35 g] pepitas to use as garnish and transfer the remaining pepitas to the prepared paper towel–lined baking sheet to cool. Add the garlic to the same now-empty skillet and cook over medium heat until lightly browned, about 30 seconds.

To the work bowl of your food processor, add the parsley, cilantro, dill, tarragon, and the cooled pepitas and pulse a couple of times until it forms a thick paste. Add the pumpkin seed oil, stir, and transfer to a small bowl. Set aside.

To prepare the vegetables: In a large bowl, combine the broccoli, cauliflower, mushrooms, garlic, olive oil, a generous pinch of salt, and several grinds of pepper and give the whole thing a stir. Spread the vegetable mixture in an even layer on the large, prepared baking sheet and roast, until the broccoli florets darken at the edges, the cauliflower gets tender, and the mushrooms soften and release some of their liquid, about 15 minutes. Transfer to a serving platter, use a spoon to spread dollops of the salsa verde across the top, scatter the reserved pepitas (for extra crunch!), and serve immediately.

SERVES 4 TO 6

Salsa Verde

¼ cup [60 ml] olive oil

½ cup [70 g] raw, shelled pepitas

½ tsp kosher salt

1 large garlic clove, smashed

¼ cup [10 g] finely chopped fresh Italian parsley leaves

¼ cup [10 g] finely chopped fresh cilantro leaves

¼ cup [10 g] finely chopped fresh dill leaves

¼ cup [10 g] finely chopped fresh tarragon leaves

¼ cup [60 ml] pumpkin seed oil

Vegetables

10 oz [280 g] broccoli crown, cut into large florets and halved

10 oz [280 g] cauliflower florets, cut into bite-size pieces (see headnote)

10 oz [280 g] cremini mushrooms, de-stemmed and halved

3 garlic cloves, minced

¼ cup [60 ml] olive oil

Kosher salt

Freshly ground black pepper

ROASTED CORN,
Spicy Mexican Style

Classic Mexican corn on the cob from a stand is smothered in mayonnaise, Cotija cheese, dried chile, and a squeeze of fresh lime—and maybe some other secret things that I don't know about. It's just so incredibly good! And it's the inspiration for this summer corn that you won't be able to get enough of. Since I gave myself the freedom to serve all kinds of non-Italian dishes at Little Owl, I knew I had to come up with a way to serve this Mexican-inspired corn I love so much (off a stick and onto a plate) at my restaurant. When the corn cools down in the husk, rotating it for a few seconds on your grill lends a little smokiness. Our Little Owl maître d' texts our neighbors (you know who you are!) to let them know when its back on my summer menu.

Preheat the oven to 350°F [180°C].

Place the corn on the center rack of the oven and roast until the husks crisp and slightly brown, about 45 minutes. Remove and set aside to cool.

Meanwhile, in a small bowl, add the mayonnaise, chili paste, lime juice, cilantro, and Parmesan cheese and mix well with a fork to combine.

Preheat your stove top grill pan over medium heat for 5 minutes.

Unhusk the roasted corn, discard the husks, and season each ear generously with salt and drizzles of olive oil. Use your hands (or a brush) to rub the olive oil all over the corn to coat them well. Place the ears on your hot grill pan and, using tongs, rotate them every 10 to 15 seconds until lightly charred all over—it happens fast; the whole grilling process should take about 1 minute.

Remove the kernels from a cob by holding the ear upright on a cutting board and running the blade of a knife down the sides of each ear. Collect the kernels and transfer to a bowl.

In a large skillet over medium heat, melt the butter. Add the corn and mayonnaise mixture and cook, stirring until evenly coated and it's all oozy melted, about 2 minutes. Transfer to a serving bowl and *devorà inmediatamente*.

SERVES 4

4 large ears corn, in the husk

3 Tbsp good, store-bought mayonnaise

1 Tbsp sambal chili paste

2 Tbsp fresh lime juice

2 Tbsp finely chopped fresh cilantro

2 Tbsp finely grated fresh Parmesan cheese

Kosher salt

Olive oil, for drizzling

1 Tbsp unsalted butter

1 lb [455 g] fresh green
beans, ends trimmed

1 Tbsp olive oil

1 Tbsp unsalted butter

1 garlic clove, minced

¼ cup [60 ml] oyster sauce

1 Tbsp sambal chili
paste (or more or less
depending on your
preference for heat)

2 Tbsp finely chopped
fresh cilantro

2 Tbsp finely chopped
fresh mint

2 Tbsp finely chopped
fresh basil leaves

1 Tbsp toasted sesame seeds

SESAME GREEN BEANS
with Mint, Chile, and Oyster Sauce

One day, while working in the back lot of Universal Studios in Los Angeles, I snooped around Chef Wolfgang Puck's makeshift kitchen that was set up in preparation for a catering event. I knew I wanted to aspire to this level of catering, so I sneaked a peek into his prep kitchen to check out how he was going to pull it all together. While snooping, I caught a glimpse of what looked like Chinese long beans with oyster sauce and sesame seeds, but I couldn't really tell, and I couldn't really ask because I wasn't supposed to be there. So I just made them! And I thought, *Oh, these are good!* And so, from that day forth, I made them my own by adding some sambal chili paste for heat, plus fresh mint, cilantro, and basil. I love the texture of the beans (we deep-fry them at Little Owl, but for home preparation, roasting in the oven achieves a nice blister), and I especially enjoy their versatility: Serve them hot as a family-style side dish or transfer to an airtight container to get cold in your refrigerator (they're wonderful served the next day alongside a piece of grilled fresh tuna). Sometimes, cooking is sneaky peeks and bursts of inspiration. I adopted these beans on a covert mission and made them my own. And now, they belong to you.

Preheat the oven to 500°F [260°C].

In a large bowl, combine the green beans and the olive oil and, using your hands, toss to coat. Transfer to an unlined baking sheet and arrange them in a single layer. Roast in the oven until the beans begin to blister slightly, 10 to 11 minutes.

In a large skillet over medium-high heat, melt the butter. Add the garlic and cook until the garlic is fragrant and lightly toasted (it can burn quickly), about 30 seconds. Add the beans, oyster sauce, and chili paste and, using a wooden spoon, gently toss the beans around in the sauce to coat them, about 1 minute. Turn off the heat and sprinkle with the cilantro, mint, basil, and sesame seeds.

Transfer to a platter (good luck resisting the urge to pick at them and eat them on the way to the table) and serve immediately. Transfer to an airtight container and store in your refrigerator for 1 day.

TENDER BROCCOLI RABE
and Toasted Garlic

SERVES 4 TO 6

½ cup [120 ml] olive oil

3 garlic cloves, thinly sliced

1½ lb [680 g] broccoli rabe, tough ends slightly trimmed but leaves left intact, cut into thirds

2 tsp kosher salt

Freshly ground black pepper

1 tsp red pepper flakes

1 lemon, cut into wedges

The old-school grand-mom secret about broccoli rabe is this: Cook it! Professional chefs want all of your vegetables to show up bright and green on your plate, so we blanch them first in hot boiling water, then shock the heck out of them in an ice-cold bath before sautéing them. But you've probably noticed, if broccoli rabe is served bright and green, it's almost always tough and bitter. You want to get it to the point where it is almost *mooshad*, which is Italian-American slang for "mushy." The Italians call it *stracotto*. And cooking it this way makes it sweet and so tender that you can spread it on a sandwich (I layer it on a roasted pork and provolone sandwich at Little Owl), mix it with scrambled eggs, toss it with leftover pasta, spread it on toast, or adorn a huge slice of Mom-Mom Pizza (page 42).

In a large skillet over high heat, warm the olive oil and add the garlic, cooking until the oil around the garlic starts to bubble and some (but not all) of the garlic pieces are lightly toasted and brown, about 1½ minutes. Add the broccoli rabe, salt, and a few grinds of pepper and cook, stirring, so that the garlic is no longer on the bottom of the skillet but is incorporated into the broccoli rabe so that it doesn't burn. Lower the heat to medium, cover with a lid, and cook for about 5 minutes.

Add the red pepper flakes, stir, turn the heat to low, and cook covered (only lifting the lid to stir now and then), about 20 minutes more. The lid traps the steam, cooking the broccoli rabe to a tender, almost "mooshad" consistency and fading that bright green bitter look to a sweeter, big love grayish green.

Transfer to a serving platter, place the lemon wedges along the dish, and serve immediately. Transfer to an airtight container and store in your refrigerator for up to 4 days.

MY EGGPLANT PARMESAN SPEECH The beauty of working with a pear-shaped vegetable is that it leaves room for irregular expression—some slices are larger, some smaller, so it's really no big whoop if you use jumbo eggplant from your garden (nice work!) or a smaller one from your grocer (also good). This recipe is forgiving, easy, and works just as well if you stack your eggplant in twos or in threes and fours—just keep the larger rounds on the bottom for stability. I've called for 1 recipe of Simple Marinara (page 106), allotting one quarter to layer your baking dish, half to layer between your eggplant slices, and the remaining quarter to garnish. But, as always, use your judgment and don't be afraid to use more or less, depending on how many stacks you yield—any leftover marinara can be reserved for later use.

SERVES 4 TO 6

2 large eggplants, about
1 lb [455 g] each, ends
trimmed, peeled, and
sliced into eighteen to
twenty-four ½ in [12 mm]
thick rounds (see note)

Kosher salt

1 cup [140 g] all-purpose
flour

3 eggs

2 cups [120 g] panko bread
crumbs

Freshly ground black
pepper

½ cup [50 g] finely grated
fresh Parmesan cheese

2 Tbsp extra-virgin
olive oil, plus more
for drizzling

½ cup [40 g] freshly grated
fontina cheese

½ cup [30 g] freshly grated
pecorino cheese

½ cup [50 g] freshly grated
aged provolone cheese

cont.

BAKED EGGPLANT PARMESAN
with Soft Herb Salad

There is an element of surprise when people discover that the baked eggplant that I serve at Little Owl is topped with a salad of soft, fresh herbs. That's an homage to our Sunday suppers, when after eating the meat course from the gravy pot, my mom would scoop a serving of salad onto the same warm, dirty plate, where it would mingle with the remnants of the gravy. The warmth of the tomato marinara sauce on the baked eggplant changes the texture of the salad, making it easier to digest and adding pleasure to the experience as you scoop up the salad along with any cheese and breading that makes its way onto the plate. Guests also seem to be surprised that it's baked, too. From a chef's perspective, eggplant is mostly made of water, and when you encapsulate it in a breading and fry it, you are essentially steaming it in its own bitter juices. It's so wrong. Baking the eggplant allows the eggplant to get crispy. And when you let it sit after removing it from the oven, the marinara has a chance to soak up the flavors of the eggplant. Salting the eggplant rounds so that they can release their bitter liquid is an essential step in the preparation. You will want to do this step 1 hour ahead of time.

Line two large baking sheets with paper towels.

Place the eggplant rounds on the prepared baking sheets, making sure they are not overlapping, generously sprinkle each round with kosher salt, and let sit for at least 1 hour.

cont.

1 recipe Simple Marinara
(page 106)

2 large handfuls arugula
and soft herbs (be joyful
about it and toss in parsley,
basil, tarragon, cilantro,
dill, fennel fronds,
chicory—whatever you
have!), roughly chopped

3 Tbsp sherry vinegar

Preheat the oven to 450°F [230°C].

Set three medium mixing bowls on your counter for a dip-and-dredge assembly line. In the first mixing bowl, add the flour. Crack the eggs into the second bowl and use a fork to lightly beat. In the third bowl, add the bread crumbs, a generous pinch of kosher salt, a few grinds of pepper, and the grated Parmesan and use your fingers to combine.

Transfer the eggplant to a large plate (they can touch now, don't worry), discard the paper towels, and wipe down the baking sheets of any excess water that was released from the eggplant.

Working with one eggplant round at a time, use a large fork to pick one up and dredge it in the flour. Shake off any excess flour back into the bowl. Next, dip it into the beaten eggs, and then finally coat it thoroughly in the bread crumb mixture. (You can also use your hands for this, but dedicate one hand for the dry dredges of flour and panko and the other hand for the wet egg dredge. Otherwise you get goopy fingers.)

Place the eggplant round back on the now-clean baking sheet. Repeat the process with each round, laying them out, evenly spaced on the baking sheets. Drizzle with olive oil and bake until lightly browned and crispy, flipping halfway through, about 4 minutes per side. Set aside to cool.

Lower the oven temperature to 350°F [180°C].

In a large mixing bowl, add the grated fontina, pecorino, and provolone and use your hands to combine.

Ladle about 1 cup [240 ml] of the marinara onto the bottom of a 9 by 13 in [23 by 33 cm] baking dish, swirling it around with the back of a spoon to spread it so that it covers the bottom to make a thin layer.

Arrange the 6 largest rounds in the baking dish. Top each one with about 1 Tbsp of the marinara sauce (using the back of the spoon to spread it around), followed by a large pinch of the cheese mixture. Stack another, slightly smaller eggplant round on top of each one and repeat the layering process of eggplant, sauce, and cheese, until each stack has three or four rounds (depending on how many slices you yielded). Finish the top with a final layer of sauce and cheese.

Bake until the cheese melts and the marinara is warmed through, about 8 minutes.

Meanwhile, prepare the herb salad. In a large salad bowl, combine the arugula, herbs, sherry vinegar, 2 Tbsp of the olive oil, a pinch of kosher salt, and two grinds of pepper. Use your hands to toss well and set aside.

Remove the eggplant stacks from the oven and use a slotted spatula to transfer the stacks to a large, beautiful serving platter.

In a small saucepan over medium-high heat, warm the remaining 1 cup [240 ml] (or more) of marinara until bubbling, about 1 minute, and spoon it over the stacks of eggplant. Divide the herb salad among the stacks, placing it in a mound on top. Serve immediately.

SERVES 4 TO 6

2 large sweet potatoes, peeled and cut into 8 to 10 uniform wedges each (see headnote)

One 12 fl oz [355 ml] can ginger ale

Packed ¼ cup [50 g] dark brown sugar

½ cup [110 g] butter, diced

OLD-SCHOOL SWEET POTATOES
and Ginger Ale

These are my mother's Thanksgiving Day sweet potatoes that we would eat starting Thanksgiving Thursday and work our way through them (with the rest of the leftovers) until Monday. Like anything "old-school," it takes you back to a time when simpler meant better. And nothing is simpler than popping open a can of ginger ale and scattering some brown sugar and butter to cook into a sweet syrup. To yield uniform wedges of potatoes so that they cook evenly, bring your potato to me and watch closely: Cut the potato in half lengthwise, then cut those halves in half, crosswise (if you have an extra-large potato, cut the pieces in half lengthwise one more time). Cutting this way ensures uniform wedges and maximum yield. It's old-school big love magic.

Preheat the oven to 375°F [190°C].

In a roasting pan, combine the sweet potatoes and ginger ale. Sprinkle the potatoes with the brown sugar and dot with the butter. Cover with aluminum foil and bake until the potatoes can be pierced easily with a fork, about 20 minutes. Uncover the pan and return it to the oven to cook until the ginger ale and brown sugar reduce by half and get syrupy and your house smells like Thanksgiving Day, another 20 minutes. Serve immediately. Transfer to an airtight container and store in your refrigerator for up to 4 days.

POTATO FONTINA FONDUTA

This rich and cheesy potato dish takes its name from the Italian *fonduta*, which is melted fontina cheese eaten with small, boiled potatoes or bread for dipping. I combine Yukon gold potatoes—love those little guys for their starchiness—with fontina cheese to make an all-in-one fonduta experience. And since I'm not fancy, you don't even have to peel them. Potato Fontina Fonduta is fantastic served alongside my Lamb T-Bones (page 163). (Here's a time management tip for that pairing: Mill the potato mixture and set it aside. While the lamb T-bones are resting, finish the preparation of the potatoes in the skillet, melting the cheeses and warming the potatoes, so that they will be good and hot and ready to serve alongside the lamb.)

In a medium saucepan over medium-high heat, add the potatoes, cover with the cream and white wine, bring to a boil, and then lower the heat to a simmer, cooking until the potatoes are easily pierced with a fork and the cream reduces a bit, about 20 minutes.

Set your food mill over a large heat-proof bowl and pass the entire contents of the pot through the mill. Transfer the milled, super-creamy potato mixture to a large skillet over medium-high heat and add the chicken broth, both cheeses, a generous pinch of kosher salt, and fresh grinds of pepper to taste, and cook, stirring, until the cheese melts and gets nice and stringy, about 30 seconds. Serve immediately.

SERVES 4

1½ lb [680 g] Yukon gold potatoes, halved or, if large, quartered

2 cups [480 ml] heavy cream

1 cup [240 ml] white wine, preferably Chablis or Sauvignon Blanc

¼ cup [60 ml] chicken broth, homemade (page 148) or store-bought

½ cup [40 g] freshly grated fontina or Gruyère cheese

¼ cup [25 g] finely grated fresh Parmesan cheese

Kosher salt

Freshly ground black pepper

2 large skin-on
Idaho potatoes

1 tsp olive oil, plus
more for rubbing

Kosher salt

⅔ cup [160 ml]
neutral oil, such as
canola or safflower

1 large leek, root end and
dark green top trimmed,
thoroughly washed, and
very thinly sliced

1 garlic clove, minced

1 generous pinch The
Harrison Spice Mix
(page 18)

2 Tbsp butter

Freshly ground black
pepper

1 Tbsp finely chopped
fresh parsley

CURRIED LEEK HOME FRIES

My home fries are perfect as a brunch side dish or served alongside my Little Owl Crispy Chicken (page 146). Following these simple rules results in extraordinary, crispy browned potatoes. First, you must get your oil smoking hot. And second, you must work in batches so as not to overcrowd the pan. When there are too many potatoes in the pan, the temperature of the hot oil drops, causing your potatoes to stick (and if they stick, you'll never achieve that venerated crispy exterior). So, patience, too, is key. Let them sizzle and fry and do their thing!

Preheat the oven to 350°F [180°C]. Line a plate with paper towels and set aside.

Using your hands, rub each of the potatoes with a generous amount of olive oil and place them on a baking sheet. Sprinkle them all over with a generous amount of kosher salt and bake until cooked through but still firm—stick a fork in one and if it comes out easily, they are done, about 1 hour. Allow the potatoes to cool before handling so you don't burn your hands off. (Ain't nothing hotter than a hot potato!) Using a sharp knife, dice the cooked, cooled potatoes into 1 in [2.5 cm] thick pieces.

In a large cast-iron skillet over high heat, heat ⅓ cup [80 ml] of the neutral oil until it smokes—you'll see a wisp of white coming off it. Working in three batches, add just enough potatoes to create a single layer, and cook until they are brown and crispy on the underside, about 2 minutes. Use a slotted spoon (or a slotted fish spatula) to flip the potatoes over and cook until the other side is brown and crispy, too, 2 to 3 minutes more.

Transfer each batch of potatoes to the prepared plate to drain any excess oil. The first two batches will absorb most of your oil, so by the time you are ready for your third batch, add the remaining ⅓ cup [80 ml] of neutral oil to the skillet before cooking them. After the final batch of potatoes, drain and discard any remaining oil from the skillet and give it a good wipe with a towel to remove any brown potato bits.

In the same skillet, add the leek, garlic, olive oil, and spice mix. Using a wooden spoon, mix to incorporate and cook until the leeks soften, about 1 minute. Return the reserved fried potatoes back to the skillet and add the butter, a generous pinch of salt, a few grinds of black pepper, and the parsley and mix it all together until the butter melts. Transfer to a platter and serve immediately.

SEASONAL
CURRIED LEEK HOME FRIES

If you'd like to jazz up your home fries to reflect the
seasons, as I do at Little Owl, add asparagus in
the spring and summer and Brussels sprouts in the
fall and winter. And of course, lobster meat anytime!
Blanching the asparagus and Brussels sprouts first
gives them a head start on their cooking time.

Asparagus Home Fries

Trim the tough ends of 12 oz [340 g] of fresh asparagus spears and cut
into 1 in [2.5 cm] diagonal pieces. Bring a large pot of generously salted
water to a boil and blanch the asparagus until bright green and tender,
3 to 4 minutes. Use a slotted spoon to transfer to the skillet and cook for
1 to 2 minutes more before adding the leeks and proceeding to the next
step. Hurray spring!

Brussels Sprouts Home Fries

Trim and quarter 2 cups [200 g] loose Brussels sprouts. Bring a large
pot of generously salted water to a boil and blanch until crisp tender,
4 to 5 minutes. Use a slotted spoon to transfer to the skillet and cook
for 1 to 2 minutes more before adding the leeks and proceeding to the
next step. Right on, it's fall!

Lobster Home Fries

Add 12 oz [340 g] cooked lobster meat to the skillet at the very end, with
the reserved fried potatoes, and toss until just warmed through, about
30 seconds. Yes, you are resplendent for making these!

CHAPTER

4

Pasta

❧ Pasta

I can write a whole other book on making fresh pasta. There is no better way to cultivate a big love for cooking than to transform some flour and eggs into beautiful pasta dough that can then be made into a fantasy of shapes, either by hand or with the assistance of a pasta maker. My big love story begins with Sunday Gravy (page 211) and homemade, fresh pasta. As a kid, nothing could match that flush of confidence that came from helping my mom-mom with her "Homemades" (page 221). And late on Saturday nights, when my mom would be busting out her pasta maker to create delicious homemade ravioli for a special Sunday dinner, my older brothers and sister would get to stay up later than me and watch reruns of *The New Adventures of Charlie Chan*. And I would be so jealous. I wanted to know what was going on with Charlie Chan, but also, what was going on with that ravioli?!

Second only to the joy I get out of cooking for others is teaching other people how to cook. And teaching people of all ages how to make fresh pasta is absolutely one of my favorite teaching experiences. But I also understand that making fresh pasta from scratch is a lifestyle choice! When you *do* have the time, be sure and open some wine, put on your favorite tunes, get the kids involved, and make it a family event. Making fresh Ricotta Cavatelli with Tomato Broth, Bacon, and Fava Beans (page 117) is so worth it. And try your hand at Baked Ricotta Crespelle (page 110)—you'll never reach for store-bought cannelloni again.

Here are a few pasta cooking tips: First, whenever cooking any pasta, fresh or dried, be sure to have ample, rolling boiling water that has been generously salted. For 1 lb [455 g] of pasta, I always recommend 2 Tbsp of fine sea salt to make your water "salty like the sea," so that while your pasta cooks, it will absorb the salt, making it more flavorful. And second, fresh pasta, homemade or store-bought, cooks very quickly, usually in less than 60 seconds, so when you see it coming up to the top of the pot, it's ready. And third, always give your pasta a few stirs while cooking. My dad loved to say, "Friends stick together—not pasta." And I think that pretty much sums up the sentiment here.

¼ cup [60 ml] extra-
virgin olive oil

4 large garlic
cloves, minced

1 large yellow onion,
ends trimmed, peeled,
and finely diced

Two 28 oz [794 g] cans
whole peeled tomatoes

2 Tbsp finely chopped
fresh basil leaves

1 Tbsp finely chopped
fresh Italian parsley leaves

1 tsp red pepper flakes

Kosher salt

Freshly ground
black pepper

SIMPLE MARINARA

I use marinara sauce in lots of dishes as a flavor glue. When I make sau-téed vegetables, such as zucchini, squash, and capers, I'll take a scoop of marinara and mix it in to add dimension, acidity, and color. Lemon juice, white wine, and vinegar need to be used sparingly or balanced with a fat or sugar element when added to a dish, but there's not enough acid in tomato marinara to curdle cream. And it can last up to 4 days in your refrigerator, so you can use it throughout the week in several dishes. If you choose to freeze your marinara and then reheat it, it will lower the acid content even more, so when reheating, throw a splash of red wine into it.

In an ample saucepot over medium-high heat, warm the olive oil. Add the garlic and onion and cook, stirring, until the garlic is lightly toasted, about 1 minute.

Pour the entire contents of the tomato cans into the pot and, using a wooden spoon, give the whole thing a few stirs. Add the basil, parsley, red pepper flakes, a generous pinch of kosher salt, and several grinds of pepper.

Turn the heat to low, cover the pot with the lid slightly ajar, and simmer, stirring now and then until the tomatoes break down (help them along by crushing them up against the side of the pot with the back of your wooden spoon) and the marinara takes on the consistency of a robustly thick tomato sauce, about 1½ hours. Cool and reserve in an airtight glass container if not using imme-diately. Store in your refrigerator for up to 4 days.

SPAGHETTI AND CLAMS

SERVES 4 TO 6

One summer, when I was ten years old, my father brought my brothers and me to the Jersey Shore and along the way he stopped and bought one hundred huge cherrystone clams. He dropped us off at our house with the clams, told us he'd be right back, and then went out drinking. Hours passed, and we grew very hungry. At some point, I decided we were going to cook the clams. I stuck them in a giant pot with water, melted some butter with garlic, tossed in some Old Bay seasoning, and waited for the clams to open. My brothers and I sat back and devoured every one of them. My father returned boozy and annoyed that we didn't save him some, but that's what he got for leaving us alone with them. For this recipe, I use the cherrystones for their gorgeous amount of liquid (clam broth or liquor) that is released when you roast them. And I love to chop the meat into hunks to toss throughout the pasta. Note: The addition of littleneck clams is optional—I love to eat spaghetti and clams without any shells in my way, but they sure do look pretty on the plate!

Preheat the oven to 400°F [200°C].

Place the clams in a large, deep roasting pan and drizzle with olive oil. Roast until the clams open completely and they release their juices, 10 to 15 minutes.

Remove the clams and transfer to a clean work surface to cool before handling—the shells will be very hot! Do not discard the clam liquid that has collected in the bottom of the pan. Set a fine-mesh sieve over a bowl and collect the juice, straining the liquid for any broken shell bits. Set aside.

Open the clams by breaking them in half and using a large spoon (I like to use the empty half of the clam shell as a scooper) to remove the meat. Using a sharp knife, chop the clam meat in the texture that is most appealing to you; I love roughly chopped, meaty hunks of clam throughout my pasta. You can chop them finer if you like. Set aside in a small bowl.

cont.

10 cherrystone clams, scrubbed and cleaned (see "Cleaning Clams," page 168)

⅓ cup [80 ml] olive oil, plus more for drizzling

3 garlic cloves, thinly sliced

4 fresh white Spanish boquerone anchovies (or in a pinch use 4 saltier, olive oil–packed anchovy fillets, drained)

½ white onion, finely chopped

2 sprigs fresh oregano, picked and roughly chopped

Pinch of red pepper flakes

½ cup [120 ml] dry vermouth

1 cup [240 ml] fresh clam juice (from cooking the clams)

½ cup [110 g] unsalted butter

1 lb [454 g] store-bought spaghetti

¼ cup [15 g] freshly grated pecorino cheese

In a large skillet over medium heat, add ⅓ cup [80 ml] of the olive oil and the garlic, warming them both until the oil shimmers and the garlic starts to sizzle, getting evenly browned and slightly toasty—give the pan a shake so the garlic doesn't stick—about 1½ minutes. Raise the heat to high, add the anchovies, onion, oregano, and red pepper flakes, and cook, stirring and breaking up the anchovies (smoosh them around with the back of your spoon to help them out) until they melt, about 1 minute.

Add the reserved clam meat and the vermouth and cook for about 30 seconds. If the vermouth catches fire, don't panic, you'll extinguish it with the clam juice. Add the clam juice and cook, letting the flavors meld and get hot, about 30 seconds. Add the butter and continue cooking until the butter completely melts and the whole mixture comes to a boil, about 1 minute. Remove the pan from the heat and set aside.

Meanwhile, bring a large pot of generously salted water to a boil and cook the spaghetti according to the directions on the package. Using tongs, transfer the spaghetti to the pan with the clam sauce, taking drips of pasta water with you. Return the pan to high heat and allow the pasta and clam sauce to get to know each other ("Hey, how you doin'?" "Good, how you doin'?" "Take me to the right place!"), bringing it back to a boil and tossing well to incorporate, about 30 seconds.

Divide among four bowls and sprinkle with the pecorino. Serve immediately.

Crespelle

3 Tbsp butter

2 eggs

¾ cup [180 ml] whole milk

1 cup [140 g]
all-purpose flour

½ tsp kosher salt

Ricotta Filling

24 oz [680 g] fresh whole-
milk ricotta cheese

1 egg

½ cup [30 g] freshly
grated pecorino cheese,
plus more for garnish

1 Tbsp finely chopped
fresh basil leaves

1 Tbsp finely chopped
Italian parsley

½ tsp red pepper flakes

Freshly ground
black pepper

3 cups [720 ml] Simple
Marinara (page 106)

BAKED RICOTTA CRESPELLE

Crespelle are thin Italian crêpes that I love to use for a lighter, more delicate version of baked manicotti. Filled with fresh ricotta and herbs and topped with my Simple Marinara (page 106), they make a gorgeous fresh-made dinner in minutes. But I also love how versatile they are: Fill them with any combo of sausage, scrambled eggs, cheeses, and asparagus, then roll them up and top them with Hollandaise Sauce (see page 46) for an Italian-style breakfast burrito. The technique for making them is so pleasurable and satisfying, it's almost addictive. I used to have to make one hundred crespelle every Friday night at the Symphony Café to prep for Saturday morning brunch, and I loved it! (I warn you, you'll find yourself in a crespelle-making rhythm screaming "ninety-nine . . . one hundred!") Let's face it, the first crespelle, just like pancakes, will always turn out to be a stinker, but once you get the hang of it, expect to yield 8 to 9 crespelle from this recipe. Note: Crespelle stay fresh for up to 2 days in the refrigerator, but because they are so light and delicate, they can dry out fast. If you plan on making them ahead of time, stack them up while cooking as directed, but before storing, brush them with 2 Tbsp melted butter and then restack them. Let them get very cold in the refrigerator before covering with plastic wrap. If you cover them before the melted butter has had a chance to solidify, it will harden and stick to the plastic, and the crespelle will break when you uncover them. Been there, done that, and it sucked.

To make the crespelle: In a small saucepan over medium-high heat, add the butter and let it melt. Continue to cook for about 2 minutes, watching carefully for these marvelous things to happen: The butter will foam and take on an amber hue, going from light tan to toasty brown. Tiny bubbles will form, and brown specks will appear on the bottom of the saucepan. You will also smell a wonderfully nutty aroma. Transfer the butter to a heat-proof bowl, leaving behind as much of the sandy flecks as you can, and let cool for 2 to 3 minutes.

Meanwhile, crack the eggs into a large bowl and gently whisk. Add the milk, ½ cup [120 ml] of water, the flour, browned butter, and salt. Gently whisk until just combined and allow to rest at room temperature, about 20 minutes.

cont.

Warm a 10 in [25 cm] nonstick skillet over medium-high heat, about 30 seconds. Remove the pan from the stove and, using a measuring cup or 2 oz [60 ml] ladle, add ¼ cup [60 ml] batter, tilting the skillet around in the air so that the batter evenly distributes and uniformly coats the bottom—it can even come up the sides a bit. Keep the skillet off the stove until the batter begins to stick and form from the residual heat of the skillet. Once formed, return the skillet to the heat and count from 1 to 10. Done. (You don't want the crespelle to brown at all—it needs to remain pliable so that you can fill and fold it).

Remove the skillet from the heat and, using a rubber spatula, loosen the crespelle around the edges and flip it, using your hands to smooth it out if necessary. Use a rubber spatula (or your hands) and slide the crespelle out of the pan and onto a large plate. As you form and stack the crespelle, they will continue to cook from the heat of one another (how nice!). Continue cooking the crespelle until you have used up all of your batter, stacking them up until ready to fill.

To make the ricotta filling: In a large bowl, combine the ricotta and egg and, using a wooden spoon, mix until well incorporated. Add the pecorino, basil, parsley, red pepper flakes, and several grinds of black pepper and mix to combine. Set aside.

Preheat the oven to 425°F [220°C]. Coat the bottom of a 9 by 13 in [23 by 33 cm] baking dish with ½ cup [120 ml] of the marinara. Set aside.

To assemble the crespelle: Using a sharp knife, cut the stack of crespelle in half, horizontally, to yield 16 to 18 half-moon shapes. Working with one crespelle at a time, spoon about 3 Tbsp [45 g] of the ricotta mixture along one edge (righties go right; lefties go left). Starting from the ricotta-filled edge, fold inward to meet the middle, sealing the ricotta. Fold over once more to meet the other side of the crespelle, creating a flat, conical-shaped package.

Place the crespelle side by side in alternating directions (they should be snuggled up to one another) and spoon 1½ cups [360 ml] of the marinara along the top of the dish, along with more sprinkles of freshly grated pecorino. Bake until the edges start to crisp, the ricotta cheese filling bubbles out a bit, and the cheese browns on top, about 15 minutes.

Divide among plates and garnish with the remaining 1 cup [240 ml] of marinara (warming it through in a small saucepan over low heat, if necessary). Serve immediately and listen to your people say, "Make these again!"

CHICKEN CACCIATORE CRESPELLE

SERVES 4 TO 6

1 recipe Chicken Cacciatore (page 149), chilled overnight

2 Tbsp finely chopped fresh Italian parsley

8 oz [230 g] fresh whole-milk ricotta cheese

½ cup [50 g] finely grated fresh Parmesan cheese, plus more for garnish

¼ cup [15 g] finely grated pecorino cheese

Kosher salt

Freshly ground black pepper

8 or 9 crespelle (see page 110), cut horizontally into half-moons to yield 16 to 18 pieces

2 Tbsp unsalted butter, melted

This recipe was born when one day, my older brother Lou, also a chef, and I were talking about how much we love to make stuffed, baked manicotti and homemade ravioli using braised meat in the filling. These chicken cacciatore–stuffed crespelle make a meal that looks like a heavy bomb but is actually sublimely light in texture while being oh-so-satiating. Did I mention that people will also think you are fancy? Here are some of our other ideas: If you love to make braised lamb, or even braised short rib, chill overnight, pick the meat off the bone, and mix it with this cheese mixture. Reserve the meat juices to spoon over the crespelle after baking. Or try topping the crespelle with Ratatouille (see page 115) for a bold Mediterranean flavor. (I love to share ideas with you!) You will want to make the chicken cacciatore 1 day in advance so you can pick the meat off the bones the next day, while it's cold.

Preheat the oven to 350°F [180°C]. Brush the bottom of a 9 by 13 in [23 by 33 cm] baking dish with olive oil. Set aside.

Transfer the chicken to a large bowl, and transfer the cacciatore sauce to a medium pot over low heat. Cook until it reduces a bit and thickens, about 15 minutes. Set aside.

Meanwhile, remove the herb bouquet from the chicken and discard. Using your hands (they are the best tool) or tongs (if you are weirded out by pulling apart chicken meat), separate the chicken from the bones—it should fall away easily—and discard the skin, bones, and any gristle you may find. The texture of the chicken should be close to shredded at this point, but if you still have largish pieces, go ahead and further break them up with your fingers or tongs. Set aside.

cont.

To the bowl of chicken meat, add the parsley, ricotta, ¼ cup [25 g] of the Parmesan, pecorino, a generous pinch of kosher salt, and a few grinds of black pepper and stir until just combined. (Don't smash it around! You want the beautiful flavors of the chicken to shine through.) Set aside.

Working with one crespelle at a time, spoon about 3 Tbsp [45 g] of the chicken cacciatore mixture onto one far edge (righties go right; lefties go left). Starting from the cacciatore-filled edge, fold inward to meet the middle, sealing the filling. Fold over once more to meet the other side of the crespelle, creating a flat, conical-shaped package.

Place the crespelle side by side in alternating directions (they should be snuggled up to one another) and brush the outside of each with the melted butter and sprinkle with the remaining ¼ cup [25 g] of Parmesan. Bake until the edges of the crespelle begin to curl and the cheese topping bubbles and browns, about 15 minutes.

Divide among plates and garnish each serving with the warmed cacciatore sauce and more sprinkles of Parmesan. Serve immediately. To store leftovers, transfer to an airtight container and store in your refrigerator for up to 2 days.

GNOCCHI
with Goat Cheese Sauce and Ratatouille

On a cold night, when you just want to get something luscious, hot, and creamy into your belly, grab store-bought gnocchi and smother it in this goat cheese sauce. Topped with a colorful, bright, and intensely flavored ratatouille, this pasta is also a crowd-pleasing dish that is perfect for a party! You can also make the ratatouille as a filling for crespelle (see page 110) or served on top of Juicy Bread (see page 169).

To make the ratatouille: In a colander set over a large bowl, add the eggplant, sprinkle with a generous pinch of kosher salt, and set aside, 20 minutes. This will help the eggplant release its liquid before cooking.

In a large cast-iron skillet over high heat, warm the olive oil until it shimmers. Add the garlic to the pan and cook until fragrant, about 30 seconds. Transfer to a large bowl. To the same pan, add the eggplant and cook, stirring occasionally, until the eggplant is softened and browned, about 3 minutes. Transfer to the bowl with the garlic. Add the onion to the pan and cook until translucent, about 1 minute. Transfer to the bowl with the garlic and eggplant.

To the same pan, add the zucchini and squash, season with a pinch of salt and black pepper, and cook, stirring, until softened and slightly browned, about 3 minutes. Transfer to the bowl with the garlic, onion, and eggplant. Add 1 to 2 Tbsp more oil to the pan, if necessary, and add the bell pepper, season with a pinch of salt and black pepper, and cook until softened and brown, 2 to 3 minutes, and transfer to the bowl with the other vegetables.

Add the tomato to the pan and cook until soft, about 30 seconds. Add the olives and capers and give them a quick stir. Add the vinegar and sugar and whisk until combined and the sugar dissolves, about 1 minute. Add the parsley and basil, stir, and transfer the whole mixture to the bowl of reserved vegetables. Stir gently to combine and set aside.

cont.

SERVES 4

Ratatouille

1 small eggplant, ends trimmed, cut into ¼ in [6 mm] dice

Kosher salt

¼ cup [60 ml] olive oil, plus more as needed

1 garlic clove, minced

1 small onion, ends trimmed, peeled, and finely diced

1 small zucchini, ends trimmed, cut into ¼ in [6 mm] dice

1 small yellow squash, ends trimmed, cut into ¼ in [6 mm] dice

Freshly ground black pepper

1 small red bell pepper, cut into ¼ in [6 mm] dice

1 whole tomato, chopped

10 black olives, pitted and roughly chopped

1 Tbsp capers, rinsed, drained, and minced

1 Tbsp red wine vinegar

½ tsp granulated sugar

1 Tbsp finely chopped fresh Italian parsley

2 Tbsp finely chopped fresh basil leaves

cont.

Gnocchi

1 lb [455 g] store-bought
gnocchi

½ cup [120 ml] chicken
stock, homemade or
store-bought

4 oz [115 g] fresh
goat cheese, at room
temperature

5 Tbsp [75 g] butter,
at room temperature

¼ cup [25 g] finely grated
fresh Parmesan cheese,
plus more for serving

Kosher salt

Freshly ground black pepper

Extra-virgin olive oil,
for drizzling

Meanwhile, to make the gnocchi: Bring a large pot of generously salted water to a boil. Cook the gnocchi according to the directions on the package. Use a slotted spoon to transfer the cooked gnocchi directly to a large skillet set over high heat. To the gnocchi, add the chicken stock, goat cheese, and butter and cook, gently shaking the pan, allowing the goat cheese to completely melt and coat the gnocchi, about 1 minute. Add the Parmesan and watch it bring the sauce together and thicken, about 30 seconds. Add a pinch of salt and a few grinds of black pepper.

Transfer the gnocchi to a serving platter and spoon the reserved ratatouille over the top. Sprinkle with more Parmesan, drizzle with olive oil, and serve immediately.

A NOTE ON CAVATELLI: Old-school grand-moms, like Rosie Bova, roll cavatelli on a little wooden board. At Little Owl, we use a hand-crank cavatelli maker (it costs about $30) to speed up the process and crank out a bajillion at a time! Store-bought or frozen cavatelli are also options in this recipe; just follow the cooking instructions on the package. If you are making same-day, fresh cavatelli, I recommend that you begin making your pasta while your tomato broth is simmering.

RICOTTA CAVATELLI
with Tomato Broth, Bacon, and Fava Beans

My cavatelli ("little hollows") are from my grandmother Rosie Bova's recipe, which mixes fresh ricotta into the dough to create tender and light little dumplings that have a wonderful toothsome texture. They float in a sweet and bracing tomato broth with bits of bacon and fresh fava beans that, to me, taste just like spring: grassy green and earthy. Capturing the taste of a season is what big love cooking is all about. The snazzy thing about this delicious, versatile tomato broth is that you can make it year-round, as I do at Little Owl. During colder weather, add some chopped Sautéed Escarole (page 233) to the broth instead. Note: The broth recipe yields about 1 cup [240 ml] more than you need. Store it in an airtight container for up to 1 week in your refrigerator. Chilled, it makes a great base from which to build a Bloody Mary, or reheat it for a late-night pasta portion for one. Or even toss a splash into some sautéed vegetables, using it for flavor and zing.

Prepare an ice water bath by filling a large bowl (preferably metal) with cold water and ice cubes. Set aside. Line a plate with paper towels and set aside.

Meanwhile, bring a large pot of generously salted water to a bowl. Add the shelled fava beans and cook until their tough outer skin softens (some of their jackets will burst) and they turn bright green, 1 to 2 minutes. Use a slotted spoon to transfer the beans to the ice water bath. Allow to cool for 3 to 5 minutes.

Now comes the fun part: Using your thumb, peel at the dimpled part of the bean so the top opens. Squeeze up from the bottom and they will push right out. Transfer them to a bowl and set aside.

cont.

SERVES 4

1 cup [120 g] fresh fava beans, shelled

¼ cup [60 ml] extra-virgin olive oil, plus more for cooking and drizzling

1 medium carrot, sliced

1 medium yellow onion, ends peeled, trimmed, and sliced

1 stalk celery, sliced

2 Tbsp finely chopped garlic, plus 1 garlic clove, thinly sliced

One 28 oz [794 g] can whole peeled plum tomatoes

6 fresh basil sprigs, plus 4 fresh basil leaves, torn

2 fresh parsley sprigs

1¼ cups [360 ml] white wine, preferably Sauvignon Blanc or Pinot Grigio

cont.

In a large heavy pot or Dutch oven over medium-high heat, warm ¼ cup [60 ml] of the olive oil, add the carrot, onion, and celery, and cook, stirring, until the carrot and celery soften and the onion becomes translucent and glassy, about 4 minutes.

Add the garlic and the entire contents of the tomato can and stir until it is warmed through, 2 minutes. Add the sprigs of basil and parsley, 1 cup [240 ml] of the white wine, and the chicken broth and bring to a boil. Lower the heat to a simmer and cook, uncovered, using a wooden spoon to give it some love by stirring occasionally, until the liquid reduces to a thick broth, about 1 hour.

Meanwhile, in a medium skillet over very low heat, add the bacon and cook, stirring occasionally, until the bacon crisps and the fat renders, about 7 minutes. Use a slotted spoon to transfer the bacon to the prepared plate to drain excess fat. Set aside.

Using a fine-mesh sieve set over a large, heat-proof bowl, strain the tomato broth by pressing it through the sieve with the back of your wooden spoon. Discard the solids. Add a pinch of kosher salt and some grinds of pepper—now taste it! The broth should be bracing and zippy, but add more salt and pepper if necessary and set aside.

Bring a large pot of generously salted water to a boil. Prepare an ice water bath by filling a large bowl (preferably metal) with cold water and ice and set aside.

Using a slotted spoon, gently place your homemade ricotta cavatelli into the boiling water and cook until they float to the top, about 1½ minutes. Use a slotted spoon to transfer them to the ice water bath to cool for 1 minute, then drain and transfer them to a clean baking sheet and drizzle with just a bit of olive oil. Let rest for 1 hour before reheating in the broth.

To prepare the dish: In a medium saucepan over high heat, add the crisped bacon, sliced garlic, and 3 Tbsp of olive oil, and cook until the garlic is toasted, about 40 seconds. Pull the saucepan away from the heat and add the remaining ¼ cup [60 ml] of white wine, 2 cups [480 ml] of tomato broth, the fava beans, and the cavatelli, stirring to combine. Add the torn basil leaves and cook, stirring and letting it come to a boil so that the cavatelli plump up in the broth and the broth reduces and thickens, about 3 minutes.

Divide among four serving bowls and top with generous sprinkles of freshly grated pecorino, drizzles of extra-virgin olive oil, and fresh cracks of pepper. Serve immediately with spoons and lose yourself in pure bliss.

2 cups [480 ml] chicken broth, homemade (page 148) or store-bought

6 oz [170 g] or about 6 slices bacon, roughly chopped

Kosher salt

Freshly ground black pepper

1 lb [455 g] fresh Ricotta Cavatelli (recipe follows)

¼ cup [15 g] finely grated pecorino cheese (I prefer Locatelli)

RICOTTA CAVATELLI

My ricotta cavatelli is very special to me and lots of Little Owl customers. And so I want you to have the recipe *exactly* how I make it. You will feel a-*freaking*-mazing! Here are a few things to keep in mind while working with this wet and sticky dough. First, the dough will be ready when (a) it no longer sticks to your hands or work surface (if it sticks to either one, it will gum up the cavatelli cutter) and (b) when it becomes slightly elastic, which means when you press a dimple into the dough with your fingers, it should bounce back at you. If you can answer, "Yes, Joey, that sounds like my dough!" after about 8 minutes of adding flour and kneading, then you're doing great! And second, between us, I never trust a fresh pasta recipe that calls for an exact amount of flour to be used. So, the amount I call for is a guideline. What I advise you to do is keep your senses engaged and feel your way through the process, adding more flour as necessary based on the conversation between you and the dough. If at any point in the process the dough feels sticky, just add a little bit of flour. Third, keep a large container or large, shallow bowl of flour close by, for rolling the cavatelli ropes before cranking them out—it's an easy, mess-free way to flour them. Finally, these cavatelli will be at their most tender and best Little Owl version if you blanch, shock, and then let them rest for 1 hour before reheating them in the broth. Right on! Let's do this!

MAKES 1 LB [455 G] CAVATELLI DOUGH, ENOUGH FOR 4 MAIN COURSES

2 cups [280 g] all-purpose flour, plus more as necessary

2 eggs, lightly beaten

16 oz [455 g] fresh whole-milk ricotta cheese

Prepare your cavatelli cutter by attaching it to your work surface and dusting the wooden rollers with a small handful of all-purpose flour. Turn the handle to pass the flour over the rollers. This will help keep the cavatelli from sticking. Place a lightly floured baking sheet in front of it to catch the cavatelli as they drop. Fill a large, shallow bowl with plenty of all-purpose flour and set it aside near your work area.

In the bowl of a stand mixer with the whisk attachment, add the eggs and the ricotta and whip until smooth, about 1 minute. Change to the dough hook attachment and slowly add 2 cups [280 g] flour until the dough begins to pull together. It will be sticky.

Generously flour a clean work surface and turn the sticky dough out onto it. Sprinkle a small handful of flour over the dough ball and, using the palms of your hands, begin to knead, using a pull, push, and turn motion. Begin by pulling the dough ball toward you, then use the heel of your hands to push the dough away, adding more flour as you do so, making sure to incorporate the flour from the work surface into the dough.

Continue kneading, adding more flour as necessary (you can easily add up to 1 cup [140 g] or more), until the dough stops sticking to your hands and the work surface and becomes slightly elastic (see headnote), about 8 minutes.

Wrap the dough in plastic wrap and set aside to rest in the refrigerator for 25 minutes.

When the dough is ready, unwrap it and place it on a lightly floured work surface. Using a pastry scraper (it's such a helpful tool when cutting pasta), divide the dough into 8 uniform wedges, just like a pie. Work with one piece of dough at time, keeping the remaining portions of dough moist under a slightly damp, clean kitchen towel.

Use a rolling pin to roll out one portion of dough into a ½ in [12 mm] thick oval. Use a pizza cutter to slice the oval into strips about ¾ in [2 cm] in width. Working with one strip at a time, roll it out into a long cable, about 18 in [46 cm] in length, with a uniform thickness. Dip the cable of dough into the prepared bowl of flour to give it a thin coating.

Feed the dough strip through the wooden rollers of the cavatelli cutter and crank away, letting cavatelli fall onto your baking sheet. As the cavatelli drop, spread them out evenly on your baking sheet (don't allow them to clump up). Repeat with the remaining dough strips and remaining 7 dough portions until you have a baking sheet with a bajillion cavatelli. Set aside until ready to use. Or cover the baking sheet tightly, all around like a package, and freeze. Once frozen, transfer to an air-tight container and store in your freezer for up to 2 weeks.

6 oz [170 g] fresh broccoli
rabe, ends trimmed

¾ cup [180 ml] Basil Pesto
(recipe follows)

Kosher salt

1 Tbsp butter

12 grape or cherry
tomatoes (a variety of
colors and sizes to
please the eye)

6 oz [170 g] pork salami
or soppressata, diced, or
deli salami, thinly
sliced into strips

1 Tbsp olive oil

1 lb [454 g] store-
bought farfalle

¼ cup [25 g] finely grated
fresh Parmesan cheese

4 oz [115 g] fresh whole-
milk ricotta cheese

Extra-virgin olive oil,
for drizzling

Freshly ground black pepper

FARFALLE
with Broccoli Rabe Pesto,
Fried Salami, and Burst Tomatoes

Farfalle ("butterflies" in Italian) is one of my favorite pasta shapes to pair with a clingy, fresh pesto sauce. For my broccoli rabe pesto, you start with my traditional Basil Pesto and add blanched and puréed broccoli rabe for an even brighter green version (it gets so green that it almost looks fake!). The addition of salty, fried salami adds texture and a subtle porky flavor that I love. Dollops of fresh ricotta cheese finish this dish to honor my dad. Growing up, he would always add a dollop of fresh ricotta to his pasta (I am more of a grated pecorino guy) and the older I got, the more I figured he was onto something. When it melts into the pasta, it's kind of big love dreamy. This pesto can be made 2 days in advance. Store in an airtight container in your refrigerator.

Prepare an ice water bath by filling a large bowl (preferably metal) with cold water and ice. Set aside.

Meanwhile, bring a large pot of generously salted water to a boil. Add the broccoli rabe and boil until it turns a bright green color and is tender, 1 to 2 minutes. Using tongs, transfer the broccoli rabe to the ice water bath and let cool for 2 to 3 minutes. Transfer to a cutting board and roughly chop. Set aside.

In the work bowl of your food processor, prepare the Basil Pesto. Add the chopped broccoli rabe and 1 tsp of kosher salt and purée until smooth, scraping down the sides to fully incorporate the mixture, about 1 minute.

In a small skillet over medium-low heat, melt the butter. Add the tomatoes and a pinch of kosher salt and cook until all the tomatoes burst open, leaking their juices into the pan, with smaller tomatoes bursting sooner, larger ones later. Not everyone always gets to the party at the same time, but they'll pop when ready, 4 to 6 minutes. Set aside.

cont.

In a large skillet over medium-high heat, add the salami and the olive oil and cook, stirring now and then, until the salami is crispy and that beautiful fatty pork smell hits your nose, 11 to 12 minutes. Transfer to a small bowl and set aside. Give the skillet a wipe to remove excess oil and set aside. (You'll use this same skillet to dress your farfalle.)

Meanwhile, bring a large pot of generously salted water to a boil. Add the farfalle, bring the water back to a boil, and cook according to the directions on the package. Before draining, use a glass measuring cup to scoop out about ¼ cup [60 ml] of pasta water (or a little more—better to have it in case you need it) and set aside.

Using a colander, drain the farfalle, shaking it to remove any visible pasta water. Transfer the farfalle directly into the now-empty and wiped-out skillet over low heat, add the broccoli rabe pesto, the Parmesan, and the reserved pasta water, and use a wooden spoon to gently and evenly coat the farfalle in creamy green pesto, alternating mixing and folding, about 1 minute. Add more pasta water, a little bit at a time (1 Tbsp constitutes a little bit, in case you're wondering), if necessary.

Transfer these gorgeously green butterflies to your favorite serving platter and serve family style, topped with the reserved salami, the burst tomatoes, and dollops of fresh ricotta. (Oh, my goodness! So nice! Like a lemon ice!) Finish with drizzles of extra-virgin olive oil and some fresh grinds of pepper. Serve immediately.

BASIL PESTO

While fresh basil pesto is a quick condiment to put together, pine nuts are expensive! Follow these tips when toasting them to protect your investment and prevent burning: (1) Always use a combination of a tiny nugget (½ tsp) of butter and olive oil. The milk solids will break down in the butter and attach to the pine nuts, giving them a really nice nutty flavor. (2) Don't walk away from the pan. And (3) lift the pan and shake while you stir (it's fun). By lifting the pan of pine nuts off the heat, you will alternate from hot to cool and toast them evenly.

MAKES ABOUT ¾ CUP [180 ML]

1 Tbsp olive oil

½ tsp unsalted butter

¼ cup [30 g] pine nuts

1 cup [12 g] packed fresh basil leaves

2 small garlic cloves

¼ cup [25 g] finely grated fresh Parmesan cheese

½ cup [120 ml] extra-virgin olive oil

Kosher salt

Freshly ground black pepper

In a large skillet over medium heat, combine the olive oil, butter, and pine nuts and toast (see headnote) until fragrant and golden brown, about 3 minutes. Transfer to a bowl and set aside.

To the work bowl of your food processor, add the toasted pine nuts, basil leaves, garlic, Parmesan, extra-virgin olive oil, a generous pinch of kosher salt, and several grinds of black pepper and spin until it makes a thick, smooth, bright green purée, about 45 seconds. Use a rubber spatula to scrape down the sides and give it another pulse to really incorporate it. If not using immediately, reserve in an airtight container for up to 1 week or divvy up the pesto in ice cube trays and freeze, taking out small portions as needed.

One 28 oz [794 g] can
whole peeled tomatoes

1 lb [455 g] pork
belly, diced

⅓ cup [80 ml] olive oil

2 Italian Long Hot peppers
or jalapeño peppers
(see headnote), roughly
chopped

2 large garlic cloves,
smashed and chopped

1 cup [240 ml] chicken
stock, homemade or
store-bought

2 Tbsp finely chopped
fresh basil leaves

1 Tbsp kosher salt

Freshly ground black pepper

1 lb [454 g] store-bought
perciatelli

¼ cup [25 g] freshly
grated pecorino cheese,
plus more for finishing

PERCIATELLI
with Spicy Pork Belly Gravy

Perciatelli, a long, thick spaghetti with a hole in it, was my mom-mom Rosie Bova's favorite pasta. And this gravy is really about the flavor of the pork fat melting and melding with the tomatoes. If you like your pork belly gravy very spicy, try using jalapeño peppers for more heat. If you prefer a shorter pasta, try rigatoni. It can stand up to the meaty pork and rich tomato flavors.

In a large bowl, add the entire contents of the tomato can and use your hands to squish the tomatoes. If you prefer a smoother texture to your sauce, use an immersion blender and give it a few whirs. Set aside.

In a large, deep skillet over medium-high heat, add the pork belly. Cook, stirring continuously, until brown and the fat of the pork belly starts to render, about 5 minutes. Use a slotted spoon to hold back the pork belly while you lift the skillet to discard the pork drippings into the empty tomato can (like my mom-mom). Add the olive oil, peppers, and garlic to the skillet and cook, stirring occasionally, until the garlic is slightly toasted and the peppers soften, about 3 minutes.

Add the reserved tomatoes and their juices, the chicken stock, 1 cup [240 ml] of water, the basil leaves, salt, and a few grinds of pepper, turn the heat to low, and cook, stirring every now and then, until the tomatoes break down, the peppers completely soften, and the pork belly flavor seeps into the tomatoes, making your house smell like heaven, 40 minutes.

Meanwhile, bring a large pot of generously salted water to a boil. Add the perciatelli, bring the water back to a boil, and cook according to the package directions, stirring now and then so that they don't stick together.

Drain the perciatelli in a colander, shaking it to remove any visible pasta water, and transfer directly to the skillet with the pork belly gravy. Add the pecorino and, using tongs, twist the pericatelli around in the skillet to incorporate the gravy.

Using tongs, divide the perciatelli among four bowls and finish with more grinds of black pepper and more pecorino. Serve immediately.

⧸⧉ TO MY FATHER, LOUIS CAMPANARO SR. ⧉⧹

My father was complicated. But aren't we all?

One of his biggest pet peeves was to see a dark red gravy spoon wind up in the pristine white ricotta container. (Look out and God forbid . . .)

Beyond ricotta, he loved fish. Sounds simple enough. And I grew up to cook for him all the fish he loved: clams, cod, stuffed flounder.

My father was a fire captain, and in one of his more complicated moves, he refused to send his battalion to their deaths in the Gulf Oil refinery fire of 1975, a blaze that burned for 6 days. From South Philly all the way up to Wilmington you could see the bright orange flames light up the sky.

My father was a drinker.

He and my uncle "ran and renovated" Scioli Turco VFW (a.k.a. The Post), a bar that proudly served members from 7 a.m. until 4 a.m. (on the days they closed!).

On special veteran holidays, my mother and aunt would send over food for the customers. Because cooking shows your love for people.

Two great things about that bar: They had (1) a pay phone as their only line of communication because, they'd say, "It's harder to tap a public phone!" and (2) a poker machine that would run videos of old, obscure horse races that you could wager on.

There were also other "fixtures" in that place, including a hall upstairs used for parties, and guys like Perpy ("Perky" to only a select few), Michael Ford, and Didee. Uncle Frankie would be there, too—either serving when he was working or being served until his next shift behind the bar.

The little wineglasses I use at Little Owl are named for him: "Uncle Frankie" glasses. The stories, the feelings, the love—so wide, so big, so *un*-complicated. White like ricotta memories.

If you know me well, you know my South Philly heart belongs to the old-school ways of my father, rough edges smoothed by the balm of my mom and mom-mom's love.

But sometimes, those old-school stories of nostalgia, heroism, and good vibes give way to some hard truths, like the time he terrified me into eating my spinach.

To this day, I still can't swallow it. But I put it on my menu, because maybe *you* like it?

My father was Louis D. Campanaro. I have so much I want to say about him.

But my memories, like him, are complicated. Like dark red gravy mingled with ricotta.

He would say, "You may as well throw the whole container away."

I say, let them live together—complicated and comingled, in memory.

MY MOTHER'S ZITI

with Cherry Tomatoes, Sausage, and Zucchini

When I was a chef at Pace in New York City in 2004, a *New York Times* restaurant critic ordered my ziti and said it was his least favorite pasta, so I got to talking to him about it afterward. I said, "How could you not like that pasta?" And he said it was very pedestrian. My reply was, "Well, yeah—my mother taught me how to make it" (awkward pause). If he only knew how often this dish wound up on our table when my mother had to feed six kids and sometimes friends and neighbors after a long day at work. It is indeed humble, fast, and delicious. If you can find only sausage links, just remove them from their casing by slicing them with a sharp knife down the middle (the casing will peel right off) and just crumble the sausage into the skillet with your hands.

In a large cast-iron skillet over medium-high heat, warm the olive oil until it shimmers and then add the crumbled sausage. Season generously with salt and pepper and cook, using a wooden spoon to crumble it further, stirring frequently, to make sure the sausage is fully browned and there are no pink parts, about 10 minutes.

Turn the heat up to high and add the sliced garlic, onion, and zucchini coins. Cook, leaving undisturbed, until the garlic gets lightly toasted and the onion begins to soften a bit, about 2 minutes. Add the entire contents of the tomato can, lower the heat to medium, and simmer all that one pan love until the tomatoes burst open, the zucchini glistens and softens a bit, the sausage gets brown in the middle, and the juices reduce by half, about 8 minutes. Remove from the heat and set aside.

Meanwhile, bring a large pot of generously salted water to a boil. Add the ziti, bring the water back to a boil, and cook according to the package directions for al dente pasta (or just taste one—if it is cooked through but has a firm bite to it, take it out; now's the time).

Drain the ziti in a colander, shaking it to remove any visible pasta water, and transfer it directly into the now-empty pasta pot over low heat. Add the reserved sausage mixture and use a wooden spoon to incorporate. Add the basil, a few grinds of pepper, and the grated cheese.

Transfer to a serving bowl and serve immediately with a big serving spoon, letting the kids fend for themselves. Transfer to an airtight container and store in your refrigerator for up to 2 days.

SERVES 4

¼ cup [60 ml] olive oil

1 lb [455 g] sweet Italian fennel sausage, casings removed (see headnote)

Kosher salt

Freshly ground black pepper

3 garlic cloves, thinly sliced

½ red onion, diced

1 medium zucchini, cut into ½ in [12 mm] thick coins

One 28 oz [794 g] can whole peeled cherry tomatoes

1 lb [455 g] store-bought ziti

4 fresh basil leaves, torn

½ cup [30 g] finely grated pecorino cheese

⫷⫸ THE GREAT PITCHFORK ⫷⫸ ATTACK OF 1890

or The History of the Campanaro Family

I guess you can say I come from a long line of people persons. Take my paternal grandfather, Antonio Campanaro. He made his living as an organ grinder in South Philadelphia and had a popular routine with a monkey on a chain named Gigi. Organ grinding with a monkey probably wasn't Nonno's dream job, but after a fight with his brother Pasquale (over a woman) escalated into an attempt by Pasquale to contaminate his brother's water well with garlic from their field, Antonio shot back with a (thankfully) failed attack on Pasquale's life with a pitchfork. And so that's how my grandfather found himself on the adventure of a lifetime. Instead of being ostracized in his hometown, he embarked on the next boat leaving the port of Termoli with the girl of his (and Pasquale's) dreams to have a fresh start in L'America! He was just one of thousands of Italian immigrants who made their way from the poverty-stricken southern regions to settle in South Philadelphia for a new life in factories, textiles, and shipyards. Or people person industries—like organ grinding. And feeding people.

A nurse comforts Gigi at Temple University Dental Clinic as my grandfather Antonio Campanaro looks on.

Béchamel Sauce

2 bay leaves

1 small whole yellow onion, unpeeled

7 fresh cloves

6 Tbsp [85 g] butter

6 Tbsp [60 g] all-purpose flour

4 cups [960 ml] whole milk

Kosher salt

Pinch of dried nutmeg

Ragù

1 medium carrot, peeled and roughly chopped

1 celery stalk, roughly chopped

1 small onion, ends trimmed, peeled, and roughly chopped

3 Tbsp plus 1 tsp olive oil, plus more for drizzling

5¼ oz [150 g] ground beef

5¼ oz [150 g] ground pork

5¼ oz [150 g] ground veal

¼ tsp cumin

Kosher salt

Freshly ground black pepper

1 garlic clove, minced

cont.

CAMPANARO FAMILY LASAGNA

My father loved ricotta cheese—so much that even if we were having riga-toni (and pretty much no one puts ricotta on rigatoni), there would always be a little on the side just for him. And he loved ricotta ravioli (especially the frozen kind from P&S Ravioli), ricotta-filled manicotti, and, of course, lasagna. My seat at the dinner table was beside him, followed by my brother Michael, my sister Michele, and my brother Louie. My mom sat directly across from him, perched at the other end of the table. And I just loved to watch him eat. Sometimes, when all other memories fall away, you are left with a singular memory that sums it all up: My father loved ricotta. And this was his favorite lasagna.

To prepare the béchamel: Attach the bay leaves to the onion, using the cloves like pushpins to hold them in place. Set aside.

In a small skillet over medium heat, melt the butter. Add the flour and whisk until absorbed and smooth, about 30 seconds. Transfer to a small bowl and place in your refrigerator to get cold. (Don't skip this step—it will keep your sauce lump-free once it's added to the warmed milk.)

In a large, deep saucepan over medium-low heat, add the milk and the onion and slowly bring it to a boil. Lower the heat to a simmer and let cook, stirring occasionally with a wooden spoon, about 15 minutes. Remove the onion and discard. Add the cold butter and flour mixture to the hot milk and use a whisk to com-bine until the milk begins to thicken and can coat the back of a wooden spoon, about 1 minute.

Set a fine-mesh sieve over a heat-proof bowl and strain the bécha-mel, using your wooden spoon to push it through the strainer and into the bowl. Add a pinch of kosher salt and the nutmeg, and stir to combine. Cover with plastic wrap, pressing it down so that it kisses the top of the sauce, preventing a skin from forming. Set aside to cool to room temperature.

cont.

¾ cup [180 ml] red wine, such as Chianti

One 28 oz [794 g] can whole peeled tomatoes

2 Tbsp finely chopped fresh parsley

Ricotta Mixture

1 egg, lightly beaten

32 oz [910 g] fresh whole-milk ricotta cheese

Kosher salt

Freshly ground black pepper

½ cup [30 g] finely grated pecorino cheese

½ cup [50 g] finely grated fresh Parmesan cheese

2 Tbsp finely chopped fresh basil leaves

2 Tbsp finely chopped fresh parsley

¼ tsp red pepper flakes

1 lb [455 g] fresh lasagna, store-bought

½ cup [50 g] finely grated fresh Parmesan cheese

To prepare the ragù: In the work bowl of a food processor, add the carrot, celery, and onion and pulse until finely chopped. Set aside.

In a large, deep skillet over high heat, warm 3 Tbsp of the olive oil until it shimmers. Add the beef, pork, veal, cumin, a generous pinch of kosher salt, and a few grinds of pepper and cook until the meat is browned, using the back of a wooden spoon to really get in there and break it up, 5 to 6 minutes.

Once the meat is browned, use your wooden spoon to move it to the side of your pan, making an empty spot in the center of your skillet. Add the garlic and cook until lightly toasted, about 30 seconds—it cooks very quickly, so be alert! Right when the garlic starts toasting, add the reserved carrots, celery, and onions and give the whole thing a stir. Stir, stir, continuously moving it around, for about 30 seconds.

Add the red wine, the entire contents of the tomato can, the parsley, and 1 cup [240 ml] of water. Lower the heat to medium and simmer, uncovered, using a wooden spoon to stir it every now and then, until it thickens, about 40 minutes. Taste and season with more salt and pepper if you think it needs it.

Preheat the oven to 350°F [180°C]. Butter the bottom and the sides of a 9 by 13 in [23 by 33 cm] baking dish and set aside. Drizzle a baking sheet with the remaining 1 tsp of olive oil and set aside.

To make the ricotta mixture: Crack the egg into a large bowl, add the ricotta, a generous pinch of kosher salt, a few grinds of pepper, the pecorino, Parmesan, basil, parsley, and the red pepper flakes. Use a wooden spoon to mix until smooth and creamy—really take about 1 minute to just mix. Add the cooled, reserved béchamel sauce to this creamy ricotta mixture to make your life of lasagna layering even easier. Set aside.

Bring a large pot of generously salted water to a boil and add the lasagna sheets. Cook according to the package directions, stirring them frequently so that they don't stick together. Lift them out of the pasta water with tongs (letting excess pasta water drip off) and transfer them to the prepared baking sheet, laying them flat and drizzling with a bit more oil. (There is nothing worse than stuck-together lasagna sheets—except stuck-together crespelle.)

In the prepared baking dish, arrange 4 pasta sheets vertically to cover the entire bottom of the dish and ladle a thin layer of the ricotta-béchamel mixture over the top, followed by a thin layer of ragù. Repeat the layering process with pasta, ricotta-béchamel mixture, and ragù until you have used up all of your components, ending with a final layer of ricotta-béchamel. Spread the top with the Parmesan.

Bake the lasagna, uncovered, until beautifully bubbly and brown on top, 45 minutes. Let rest for 30 minutes before serving so that the sauce sets and doesn't spill out when you slice it and serve it to *your* dad. Allow any leftover lasagna to cool completely in the baking dish before transferring to an airtight container and storing in your refrigerator for up to 2 days. Alternatively, if you have a lot of lasagna left over, just leave it in the baking dish and wrap tightly with plastic wrap before storing.

CHAPTER
5
Meat and Poultry

🪶 Meat and Poultry

Back in the day, going to Guerrera's butcher shop on Eighth and Catharine was always very intimidating, most especially Vito the butcher's gigantic hands (and pristine lab coat). He was powerful and meticulous when cutting the meat to order. And then he would lazily wrap up a piece of meat in butcher paper and tie it with string, not giving a care that so many people were waiting in line. It was one speed and he was in charge. But for all the intimidation, it was a curious world that I knew I wanted to enter. I would make little designs in the sawdust with my feet while gawking at the knives that were worn down from being grinded so much; pounding scaloppine for a classic, tender, melt-in-your-mouth Veal Marsala (page 157); and trimming heavy layers of fat. I also loved his butcher block that had a bevel in it from years of being used. I especially appreciated the fact that we would never have to pull a "next in line" number because my mom and mom-mom got preferential treatment.

When sourcing meat, I encourage you to rely on your local butcher. Ask them to prepare my recommended custom blend, and relish in a Little Owl Bacon Cheeseburger (page 51) at home! They want us to be curious, captivated, and excited—about their knowledge, their unique world, and family-owned farms. And I guarantee that your local butcher has stellar thick cuts of lamb for my Lamb T-Bones (page 163), which carry a depth of flavor akin to a T-bone steak! They can answer questions about primal cuts of meat (most big-box grocery stores will not break down a whole animal the way a craftsman butcher can) and why some cuts that save you money are excellent choices to capture big flavor, like my Sangria-Marinated Skirt Steak (page 160). Bring home a beautiful air-chilled whole bird to make my Little Owl Crispy Chicken (page 146). Or embrace duck fat to make a gorgeous, perfectly delectable Long Island Duck Breast with Cherries and Arugula (page 153) for your next party! And there is nothing like weaving an easy, one-pan dish such as my Salad Dressing Chicken with Escarole and White Beans (page 142) into your weeknight lineup. Go forth and find *your* Guerrera's!

LITTLE OWL LOVE NOTES When we present a check to our guests at Little Owl, we place it in a blank notebook that quickly fills up with love notes, like these: "I came here with a handsome chap whom I met three nights ago . . . He lied about his age and name—Marco, 27. He was neither. But the sliders were so delicious I did not care." Or "Dahlia wanted to air some grievances for areas I screwed up in. And I think we're OK now. The pork chop helped. Thanks." Or even a haiku poem like this one:

We came here for brunch.
So much city goodness—yum—
coming back for dins! —Cait & Suey

But one day I came across a note addressed to me:

Dear Joey Campanaro,
Your cavatelli pasta & Mexican corn were wonderful, but I ordered chicken livers & got chicken liver pâté instead. I didn't complain at the time & never do which would ruin a nice evening. But the "chicken livers" were too much to forgive. Having eaten all over the world for 35+ years & being one who truly enjoys trying everything, I have never been more disappointed & this is my first complaint I have ever made.

So, I looked up his reservation and called him and explained that the dish says mousse on the menu and I was so sorry that he was disappointed. (I didn't dare tell him that I put cream cheese in it, too.)

CHICKEN LIVER MOUSSE

SERVES 4 TO 6

2 cups [400 g] large chicken livers, drained and patted dry with paper towels

Kosher salt

Freshly ground black pepper

3 Tbsp neutral oil

1 large shallot, thinly sliced, about ½ cup [50 g]

3 sprigs fresh thyme, finely chopped

1 Tbsp butter

cont.

My chicken liver mousse contains Philadelphia cream cheese (what!) because, after all, I am a creature from South Philly. In having fun with traditional things on my menu, I've discovered the addition of Philly cream cheese makes it light and airy. And it makes it mine. You may find that you are eating it by the spoonful. Oh, and this dish doesn't pretend to be related to sautéed chicken livers and onions. I hope *you* forgive me.

Generously season the livers with salt and pepper. Set aside.

In a large cast-iron skillet over high heat, warm the oil until smoking. Carefully place the chicken livers in the skillet, being careful not to overlap or crowd them—these little guys need their space to cook evenly. Let them sit and cook on one side, until they get some brown color on their undersides, about 30 seconds. Add the shallot, thyme, and butter, give a big stir, then continue to cook, stirring occasionally, until the livers brown all over, the butter melts, and the shallot softens, about 3 minutes more.

Add the red wine and let it bubble and cook, stirring and watching for the wine to reduce by more than half and keeping an eye out for the livers to release their blood, which will thicken the whole mixture and give the remaining liquid in the pan an almost syrupy texture, about 4 minutes.

Transfer the mixture to the work bowl of your food processor, using a wooden spoon to stir and scrape up any browned bits left behind, add the cream cheese, and blend until creamy, about 30 seconds.

Set a fine-mesh sieve over a large bowl, and using the back of a wooden spoon, pass the mixture through by swirling it with the back of your spoon to remove any lumps and achieve a light texture. Transfer to an airtight container, pressing a piece of plastic wrap over the mousse so that it kisses the surface. Cover with the lid and refrigerate overnight.

Serve slathered on toasted crusty bread and top with cornichons and Pickled Red Onions (page 84). To store, transfer to an airtight container, pressing a piece of plastic wrap over the mousse so that it kisses the surface. Or spoon over a layer of duck fat (see page 151). This will prevent it from drying out and also prevents oxidation, which will discolor your mousse. Cover tightly with a lid and store in your refrigerator for up to 2 days.

½ cup [120 ml] dry red wine, such as Chianti

2 oz [55 g] Philadelphia brand cream cheese, at room temperature

4 bone-in chicken quarters (skin-on chicken legs with thighs attached), about 3 lb [1.4 kg]

Kosher salt

Freshly ground black pepper

¾ cup [180 ml] Sherry Shallot Vinaigrette (page 69)

One 15 oz [425 g] can cannellini beans, rinsed and drained

½ lb [230 g] escarole, bathed and chopped (see "How to Give Your 'Schka-Role' a Bath," page 67)

1 fresh dill sprig, roughly torn

1 fresh tarragon sprig, roughly torn

1 Tbsp roughly chopped fresh Italian parsley

SALAD DRESSING CHICKEN
with Escarole and White Beans

This is just the kind of dish my mom, Patricia, would make—delicious, quick, plentiful, and pretty hands-off; just pop it in the oven and an hour later it's done, which makes it a perfect weeknight dinner. Selecting chicken legs with the thighs attached ensures that they have a good amount of fat so they stay juicy. When they cook and release their fat and juices, they mingle in the pan with the Sherry Shallot Vinaigrette, creating a mixture that's reminiscent of a hot mustard dressing. Once you get some heat on the escarole from the warmth of the salad dressing, it wilts slightly and the bitterness fades. And who doesn't love a flavor burst of fresh herbs in the salad?

Preheat the oven to 375°F [190°C].

Place the chicken legs in a large baking dish and season them generously on both sides with salt and several grinds of pepper. Pour the vinaigrette over them and bake, uncovered, until their juices run clear and the skin crisps, about 1 hour.

Meanwhile, in a large mixing bowl, add the beans, escarole, dill, tarragon, parsley, a generous pinch of salt, and more grinds of pepper. Using your hands, toss everything together until combined. Cover with a damp paper towel to keep everything crisp and cool. Set aside.

Remove the chicken legs from the oven and tilt the baking dish carefully over the beans and escarole mixture, pouring half of the hot dressing from the baking dish into the bowl. Set the baking dish aside. Using tongs, toss the escarole and beans with the hot dressing until the escarole begins to wilt a bit from the heat.

To serve, divide the escarole and beans among four plates and place a chicken leg on top. Using a whisk, combine the remaining vinaigrette mixture in the pan, spoon over each portion, and serve immediately. (Hot dang, that was easy!) Transfer any leftovers to an airtight container and store in your refrigerator for up to 2 days.

Music and cooking go hand in hand for me—I get inspiration and energy from eclectic mixes of songs ranging from reggae, Led Zeppelin, Guru, Prince, Vicente Fernández, and Frank Sinatra. And at Little Owl, we are known for our transporting playlists created by our maître d', Chris Root. You can find them on Spotify by searching "Little Owl loves . . ." (rain, wine time, mellow jazz, Brazilian funk, misses Prince, fireplace favorites, Mr. Bojangles—yes, ten versions of that favorite song). Type in anything you can think of and we probably have it.

LITTLE OWL LOVES

A GREAT PLAYLIST

1963	**Young Americans**	**Yellow Submarine**
New Order	David Bowie	The Beatles
Your Time Is Gonna Come	**49 Bye-Byes**	**Word Up**
Led Zeppelin	Crosby, Stills & Nash	The Hit Crew
200 More Miles	**You're So Vain**	**9 to 5**
Cowboy Junkies	Carly Simon	Dolly Parton
Your Mother's Son-in-Law	**You Send Me**	**Swingin' Party**
Billie Holiday	Aretha Franklin	The Replacements

HOW TO BUTCHER
A LITTLE OWL CRISPY CHICKEN

Did you know that butchering a whole chicken is an empowering and enriching kitchen skill to have? You'll save money (by weight, a whole chicken costs much less than chicken parts) and you'll grow by leaps and bounds in kitchen confidence. Learning to butcher one chicken means you're on your way to being capable of butchering four other birds: turkey, duck, quail, and Cornish game hen—they share a similar anatomy. It will make you feel like the master of your own kitchen universe!

And inherent in my Little Owl butchering technique are a couple more wonderful things: You get to cook the Little Owl Crispy Chicken (page 146) at home and you get a fabulous homemade broth (page 148) out of the deal (using the leftover chicken carcass and wings). Nervous? Here's a pep talk: A very sharp knife, practice, and fortitude are key when butchering any animal. If you think you're going to cut yourself, you will. So just don't think those thoughts. Proceed slowly and feel your way through the process, simply guiding the knife and letting the blade do the work. So, let's get this bird ready.

MAKES 2 PORTIONS
PLUS LEFTOVER MEAT FOR CHICKEN BROTH

1. Place the chicken breast-side up on a clean work surface with the legs facing you. Grab a wing and use a sharp boning knife to gently score the joint of the wing bone, on either side, right at the point where it connects to the breast (some people may call it the shoulder). Hyperextend the wing bone and pull it off. It should yield a perfectly clean bone (the airline bone). This is left intact for pretty presentation. Repeat this step on the other wing.

2. In order to maintain the skin on the breast, thigh, and drumstick, pull the chicken close to you (so close it almost touches your belly), before proceeding with the butchering.

3. Now, place one hand at the top of the bird, and gently push, applying pressure to one side of the breast. Gently insert your knife until you feel the breastbone and score all the way down the chicken. Use your hands and pull the meat back, reinserting your knife along the rib cage, beginning to cut as far back as the wish bone. Hold your knife at an angle and let the blade do the work as you feel it slice through the rib cage and cartilage. Cut along the bone, slicing right down the center through to the thigh until you reach where the hip meets the back of the chicken. Hyperextend the thigh, pulling back, until you can see it pop out of the hip joint.

It's smooth sailing from here.

4. Grab the airline wing bone that is sticking out of the breast and, using it as a marker, locate its joint on the cavity side of the bird. Cut through that joint to disconnect it. Next, continue cutting on the cavity side of the hipbone until you can clearly separate the thigh and drumstick from the bird. They will remain connected to the breast by a sheet of skin (that you are going to get beautifully brown and crispy). This is your first portion of half chicken. Repeat the process on the other side. Once you have both portions, let's debone the thigh and drumstick.

5. Using your knife, follow and cut along the leg and thighbone on either side to expose the femur. Carefully insert the knife where the leg would meet the chicken foot. You can hold on to the leg bone and the thighbone at the same time, holding them upright and letting gravity help you, gently scraping down with your knife, being careful not to break the skin and pull the bones. (By the way, once completely scraped, you'll see that their juncture is what would be the chicken knee.) Discard the bone and repeat the process with the remaining half of chicken (turn the chicken around, unless you are ambidextrous like my business partner, Chef Mike Price) to yield the second portion.

6. Trim off any excess fat along the edges of the breast and reserve, transferring it, along with the wings and carcass, to an airtight container to use for Homemade Chicken Broth (page 148).

SERVES 2

One 3 lb [1.4 kg] air-
chilled whole chicken,
butchered into two
portions, the Little
Owl way (see page 144)

Kosher salt

Freshly ground white pepper

⅓ cup [80 ml] neutral
oil, such as canola
or vegetable oil

1 lemon, halved

LITTLE OWL CRISPY CHICKEN

In my opinion, Chef Johnathan Waxman is the best person ever to cook a chicken. Period. But I have to admit, I also have a way with chicken that people crave at Little Owl. My guests are always wowed by this boneless swathe of white meat and dark meat bound by a marvelous sheet of crispy chicken skin. There are two secrets to this flavorful, juicy bird: First, I recommend looking for an excellent-quality, air-chilled organic whole chicken or chicken parts such as ones from Bell & Evans farm. Air-chilling evenly distributes cold temperature and doesn't add extra moisture (which gets absorbed into the tissues of the bird and destroys the possibility for deep chicken flavor and crispy skin). "But, what if I see a lovely bird kept on ice at the farmers' market, Joey?" Be wary of buying chicken that is kept cold on ice. Ice doesn't evenly cool a chicken—at worst it can burn a bird in spots and create warm spots in others, sending a chicken straight into the temperature danger zone for bacterial growth. And second, you must start off cooking your chicken in a smoking-hot skillet to crisp the skin and then transfer it to your super-hot oven, keeping it skin-side down. (This was a very passionate chicken speech. Now, get cookin'!)

Preheat the oven to as high and as hot as it can possibly go—I mean it.

Place the prepared chicken on a clean surface, skin-side up. Season generously with salt. Turn the chicken over, making sure to move the chicken breast tenderloin over (it's like a little flap) to bridge the gap between the thigh meat and the breast meat, creating a perfectly even sheet of meat, and season generously with salt and white pepper.

In a large, ovenproof skillet (wide enough to hold two portions of chicken without overcrowding) over high heat, add the oil and heat until it smokes.

Remove the skillet from the heat, tilt it away from you, and gently, calmly, and nicely place a portion of chicken in the pan, skin-side down. (Don't throw it in the pan, fancy pants, or you'll get splashed with oil and burn yourself or your special somebody standing next to you.) Listen to that sizzle! Immediately add the second portion the exact same way. Give the pan a little shake and then transfer it to the oven, cooking them on one side only, until the skin is crispy, the flesh begins to brown, and the juices of the meat run clear, about 8 minutes. Serve immediately with a lemon half and Curried Leek Home Fries (page 100).

1 chicken carcass

2 chicken wings

Leftover chicken fat
from butchering

1 large carrot, peeled,
roughly cut into large coins

4 stalks celery, roughly
chopped, leaves and end
pieces discarded

1 large white onion,
ends trimmed, peeled,
and quartered

3 large garlic cloves, peeled

45 whole black peppercorns

2 whole cloves

1 fresh bay leaf

1 large sprig fresh thyme

HOMEMADE CHICKEN BROTH

You butchered a chicken (see page 144)? Right on! Take that carcass and spin it into a fantastic broth for your homemade soups. The most important thing I want you to remember is that a chicken broth should come to a boil only long enough to remove the impurities from the top. Allowing it to boil longer results in a potentially grainy (from bone fragments) and cloudy broth, which is unpleasant in both look and taste. (And in my world, unprofessional!)

In a large stockpot, add the chicken carcass, wings, chicken fat, carrot, celery, onion, garlic, peppercorns, cloves, bay leaf, and thyme. Add 12 cups [2.8 L] of water and set it over very high heat to come to a boil.

As the broth starts to warm, you'll notice the top of it takes on a bluish, hazy tint. Once it comes to a boil, use a ladle and scoop out all the fat and impurities that float to the top (the scum!). That scum is actually the blood of the chicken coagulating and cooking. If you have a dog, add a bit of the scum to their dry dog food and they will love it. (Big love is for pets, too.) Otherwise, get rid of it. Boil the broth only long enough to remove the fat and scum at the top, then reduce the heat to a simmer and cook for 1 hour.

Set a fine-mesh sieve over a large heat-proof bowl and strain the broth. Discard the solids that collect at the bottom. Your broth should be clear—a clear broth is a tasty broth.

Transfer to a heat-proof container and refrigerate. Once cool, you can freeze for up to 3 months in any size container you like (including ice cube trays, for times when you may need only a small portion of broth for a recipe).

CHICKEN CACCIATORE

Chicken cacciatore takes its name from the Italian word for "hunter." And this recipe captures the essence of a slow-cooking technique that yields woodsy, earthy, herbal flavors. To reach a sublime depth of flavor, I recommend that you use skin-on, bone-in chicken thighs. Or if you prefer, you can also use drumsticks or wings (although they yield less meat to pick off, they are delicious). It's so good to serve alongside buttered noodles or rice and some wonderful, garlicky sautéed spinach. (I'll pass on the spinach, thank you, but I hear it's delicious.) And my favorite part about chicken cacciatore is that it makes an incredible filling for Chicken Cacciatore Crespelle (page 113) when prepared 1 day in advance and chilled overnight in your refrigerator. I love you and want you to be happy however you want to enjoy this dish!

Preheat the oven to 375°F [190°C].

Gather the thyme, rosemary, and bay leaves into a bundle and tie them together using unwaxed kitchen string for an herb bouquet. Set aside.

Generously season the chicken with salt and pepper on both sides. Place the flour in a large, shallow bowl and, using tongs, dredge the chicken pieces in the flour, one at a time, gently shaking off any excess back into the dish. You want enough flour on the chicken to thinly coat it (you don't want any clumps of flour clinging to it). Transfer to a plate and set aside.

In a large, shallow brazier pan (if you have one) or a large Dutch oven, with enough surface area to fit the chicken, warm the canola oil over high heat until almost smoking. Add the chicken skin-side down and cook for 1 minute, then lower the heat to medium-high and continue cooking until the skin is browned, 3 to 4 more minutes. Using tongs, carefully turn the chicken over and cook until the underside is brown, too, an additional 3 minutes. Transfer to a plate and set aside.

cont.

SERVES 4

3 fresh thyme sprigs

3 fresh rosemary sprigs

3 fresh bay leaves

2 lb [910 g] bone-in, skin-on chicken thighs

Kosher salt

Freshly ground black pepper

½ cup [70 g] all-purpose flour, for dredging

¼ cup [60 ml] canola oil

¼ cup [60 ml] olive oil

3 garlic cloves, sliced

1 large carrot, peeled and cut into ½ in [12 mm] dice

2 stalks celery, cut into ½ in [12 mm] dice

1 medium white onion, ends trimmed, unpeeled, and cut into ½ in [12 mm] dice

1 lb [455 g] assorted mushrooms (my go-to mix is cremini, shiitake, and oyster), tough ends discarded, cut into bite-size pieces

½ cup [45 g] black olives, pitted

One 28 oz [794 g] can diced tomatoes

1 cup [240 ml] white wine, preferably Sauvignon Blanc or Pinot Grigio

Discard the cooking oil, leaving any bits of chicken stuck to the pot, and return the dirty pot to the stove. In the same dirty pot over medium-high heat, add the olive oil and warm until it shimmers (it won't take long—that pot is hot!). Add the garlic and cook until it is toasty and fragrant, 1 to 2 minutes. Add the carrot, celery, and onion and cook until the carrot and celery soften and the onion is translucent, 5 to 6 minutes. Return the now nicely browned, beautiful chicken thighs to the pot and add the herb bouquet, mushrooms, olives, the entire contents of the tomato can, the white wine, and just enough water so that the chicken floats (do not submerge it!) Cover with a lid, transfer to the oven, and cook until the chicken easily pulls apart from the bone and the liquid is reduced, about 1 hour and 15 minutes.

Discard the herb bouquet. Transfer the chicken to a large, deep serving platter or dish and top with all the hearty, rustic, and flavorful juices to enjoy family style. Serve immediately.

EMBRACE THE FAT

YOU

"My duck is tough and dry and tasteless,
and now my dinner is ruined."

ME

"You need to embrace the fat."

YOU

"You want me to hug my duck, Joey?"

ME

"Not literally—just accept that duck is poultry, not red
meat. So, the fat isn't marbled, and it won't keep the
meat juicy, like a steak. And, it's thicker than the fat and
skin on a chicken, so you need to season it aggressively!"

YOU

"Go on."

ME

"Season so much that you can see a thin layer staring
back at you, because that incredible layer of fat will
cook and render, and most of the seasoning will melt
off. Also be sure to lower the heat and cook it slowly.
Too-high heat dries it out and makes it look like that
rubber shoe you're holding in your hand."

YOU

"That's not a shoe, it's my duck."

ME

"Sorry. Well, do you want to start over with my simple
recipe for Long Island Duck Breast with Cherries and
Arugula, a fresh perspective, and a newfound vision for
rolling with duck breast like a boss? I think you can do it."

YOU

"You think I can do it?!"

ME

"I *know* you can do it!"

LONG ISLAND DUCK BREAST
with Cherries and Arugula

SERVES 6 TO 8
AS AN APPETIZER

¼ cup [30 g] slivered almonds

¼ tsp butter

2 Long Island duck breasts (about 10 oz [280 g] each), patted dry with a paper towel

Kosher salt

Freshly ground black pepper

6 oz [170 g] arugula

¼ cup [25 g] finely grated fresh Parmesan cheese

¼ cup [60 ml] Sherry Shallot Vinaigrette (page 69)

1 tsp white truffle oil

4 oz [115 g] fresh cherries, pitted, or dried cherries

Maldon sea salt flakes

As a chef, I love sharing knowledge to help you get over any cooking fears. And duck breast can create kitchen intimidation; you want to cook it at home, but you fear it. Because, when overcooked, it's one of the most unforgiving meats imaginable. The truth is, it is very easy to cook duck once you embrace the fat and season it properly (see "Embrace the Fat," page 151). Long Island duck breasts are tender, mild in flavor, and not as large as a common Moulard duck breast, so they cook faster. And when thinly sliced, they make this lovely salad that is simple to assemble yet looks so fancy on the plate. Pairing a bit of sweet fruit is always delightful to offset the rich gaminess of duck, and the possibilities are endless! I love fresh cherries in early summer and dried cherries in the winter months. Sweet blueberries dazzle in this salad, too, if they float your boat. Note: Because you are cooking this slowly, you'll render a clear, clean duck fat in your pan that you can pour off and spoon over the top of your cooled Chicken Liver Mousse (page 140) instead of plastic wrap, so that once the fat hardens, it becomes a natural sealant, preventing oxidation.

In a small skillet over low heat, add the slivered almonds and the butter. Gently toast, stirring frequently (don't walk away!) until golden, about 3 minutes. Transfer to a bowl and set aside.

Using a sharp knife, make a small crosshatch pattern across the skin of the duck. Be gentle and do not cut through to the meat. Aggressively season the duck breast skin with salt and pepper (see "Embrace the Fat," page 151) and place it skin-side down in a cold, heavy cast-iron skillet and turn the heat to medium. Cook, rendering the fat of the duck breast slowly and gently until the skin turns golden brown and crispy, 5 to 6 minutes.

Using tongs, carefully turn over the breast and cook skin-side up for an additional 4 minutes. Transfer to a plate and allow to rest for about 10 minutes so that the duck retains all of its flavorful juices.

Meanwhile, in a large mixing bowl, combine the almonds with the arugula, Parmesan, vinaigrette, truffle oil, and cherries. Using tongs, toss until well combined.

Transfer the salad to a beautiful serving platter, spreading it out so that it makes a lovely bed on which to rest the sliced duck. Using a very sharp knife, thinly slice the duck breast and drape the slices across the top of the salad. Sprinkle with Maldon sea salt flakes. Serve immediately.

LET'S TALK PORK We've come a long way from the days of overcooked dry pork and applesauce. Yet some folks still have a hard time consuming a piece of pork that has the slightest hint of pink. But, I promise you, the days of trichinosis are over. The presence of trichinae parasites has been virtually eliminated in the United States due to best farming practices. Since 2006, I've been using a double-cut 14 oz [400 g] Berkshire pork chop from Pat LaFrieda Meat Purveyors. Pat works with a coalition of independent family-owned farms in the Midwest that humanely raise Berkshire pigs that are given room to roam and are antibiotic-free. At Little Owl, I cook my pork chop to an internal temperature of 145°F [63°C], or medium-rare, to yield tender and juicy meat. I recommend you do the same. Also, choosing a double cut of pork for this recipe with a nice band of fat is key. When the fat renders, whatever seasoning was on the meat comes off, so don't be afraid to be generous with the salt.

SERVES 4

1 Tbsp fennel seeds

4 large garlic cloves, minced

¼ cup [60 ml] extra-virgin olive oil, plus more for drizzling

Four 14 oz [400 g] pork rib chops, 1½ in [4 cm] thick

1 lb [455 g] dried, large white beans, such as gigante, soaked overnight and drained, or one 15½ oz can [445 g] white beans, such as butter beans or cannellini, thoroughly rinsed and drained (see headnote)

1 lb [455 g] smoked ham hock

cont.

LITTLE OWL PORK CHOP
with Parmesan Butter Beans

Little Owl is a destination for my pork chop. People come from all over the world to experience this huge, tender, scrumptious piece of meat in our tiny room (and it's been on our menu from the day we opened our doors!). The success of the dish begins with the quality of the pork and just three ingredients in the marinade: extra-virgin olive oil, fennel, and garlic, each working in harmony to draw out every bit of juicy goodness in your pork chop. And the beauty of this recipe is that you can get a great caramelization on a small stove top griddle before finishing the pork in the oven. If you prefer to use canned beans (butter beans or cannellini beans work well), go for it! Just thoroughly rinse them to get as much salt off them as you can. When it's time to heat them through, substitute ¼ cup [60 ml] chicken stock for the bean liquid in the method. Yes, you'll miss out on the hint of smoky ham hock, which has an incomparable depth of flavor, but that's life. I still want you to have an alternative. And that pop of pickled fennel in the salad complements the fennel seed in the marinade. It's such a lovely flavor surprise and makes the Little Owl Pork Chop stand apart from the rest. Don't skip it! Note: This recipe calls for marinating the pork, preparing the Pickled Fennel (page 85), and soaking the beans overnight.

cont.

1 medium carrot,
halved crosswise

1 stalk celery,
halved crosswise

1 small onion, ends
trimmed, peeled,
and halved

1 large pinch The Harrison
Spice Mix (page 18)

Freshly ground black pepper

2 Tbsp butter

¼ cup [60 ml] chicken
stock (if using canned
beans), homemade
(page 148) or store-bought

¼ cup [25 g] finely grated
fresh Parmesan cheese

1 Tbsp finely chopped
fresh Italian parsley

4 oz [115 g] dandelion
greens, trimmed (about
2 packed cups)

7 or 8 slices Pickled Fennel
(page 85)

2 Tbsp Sherry Shallot
Vinaigrette (page 69)

Maldon sea salt flakes

In a small bowl, combine the fennel seeds, garlic, and ¼ cup [60 ml] of the olive oil. Place the pork chops in a large glass baking dish and rub the garlic-fennel mixture over the pork chops. Cover tightly with plastic wrap, sealing it like a package, and refrigerate overnight.

In a large saucepan, place the beans, ham hock, carrot, celery, and onion and cover with 3 in [7.5 cm] of water. Bring to a boil over medium heat. Reduce the heat to low and simmer until the beans are tender, about 1½ hours. Let the beans cool in the liquid, then drain, reserving ¼ cup [60 ml] of the cooking liquid and discarding the vegetables and ham hock. Set the beans aside.

Preheat the oven to 375°F [190°C].

Prepare a stove top grill pan by brushing it with a splash or two of neutral oil (alternately, splash the corner of a clean kitchen towel with a bit of oil and rub it all over the grill pan). Preheat over medium heat for 5 minutes.

Generously season the pork chops with sprinkles of The Harrison Spice Mix and grinds of pepper, making sure to aggressively season any layer of fat that may be around the pork (the fat will melt, and some seasoning will fall off on the grill pan).

Place the pork chops on the grill pan and grill for 2 minutes on one side. Using tongs, carefully flip and grill the other side for 2 minutes more. Transfer to a baking dish and cook until the internal temperature is 145°F [63°C], 8 to 10 minutes. Remove from the oven and let rest for 5 to 10 minutes.

Meanwhile, in a large skillet over medium-low heat, melt the butter. Add the beans and the reserved cooking liquid (or chicken stock, if using canned beans) and cook over medium-low heat until the beans are warmed through and nicely glazed, about 2 minutes. Stir in the Parmesan and parsley and continue cooking and stirring until the cheese melts and the beans are thick and creamy, about 2 minutes more. (Canned beans may need an extra 1 to 2 minutes of stirring to reach that thick consistency.) Set aside.

In a large bowl, combine the dandelion greens, pickled fennel, and vinaigrette. Use your hands to mix well and set aside.

Divide the beans among four plates and top each with a pork chop. Place a little mound of the dandelion green salad on top and finish with drizzles of extra-virgin olive oil and a few Maldon sea salt flakes. Serve immediately and say "Wowie!"

FOR THE OLD-SCHOOL KITCHEN GUYS IN SOUTH PHILLY: Hey, you, with the cigarette hanging off the kitchen pass! I see your *veal deal*.

Your red sauce joint is jumping on a busy Saturday night and I know you need those kitchen burners in your tiny kitchen (mine's tiny, too!) for so many of your Italian-American delights—Pasta with Broccoli! Flounder Francese! Chicken Piccata!

I watch your kitchen tongs clasp the edges of your floured veal scaloppine as you dip them into a huge, deep saucepot full of olive oil that's warmed just enough to seal the deal.

I see you lay 'em down to cool, then stack 'em up high like playing cards until . . .

Ding! (order in)

And you deal out your cold veal into a saucepan filled with hot, buttery Marsala sauce.

Only three minutes later, Mr. & Mrs. on table 5 are digging in!

I gotta tell you old-school guys . . .

This ain't a cooking technique I recommend.

(But I admire your stone-cold old-school cooking shortcut.)

VEAL MARSALA

My favorite Italian-American South Philly dish (besides Sunday gravy) that I crave and make at home is veal Marsala. With so few ingredients, it's a quick weeknight meal, and when done well, it's fantastic. The addition of a spoonful of veal demi-glace in my recipe gives it a depth of flavor and appearance that is glossy and smooth. You must use a good, dry Sicilian Marsala (dry is best for this recipe, but if you have only sweet on hand, go for it) so that the distinct, nutty, complex flavors of this fortified wine shine through. Conversely, if you use sweet Marsala, your sauce will pick up the flavors of molasses and caramel that dominate the sweet version. Also, dry Marsala is a wonderful aperitivo, so you can sip 'n' cook. My go-to mix for a mushroom medley in all of my recipes is a blend of fresh shiitake, cremini, and oyster mushrooms. Together, they have a balanced earthiness and I love the meaty body and texture. Note: Most grocery stores sell veal already sliced and pounded into scaloppine, Italian for "little slices of meat." The cut of scaloppine is from the top round, which is from the top inside of the veal leg, so it may be packaged as veal leg for scaloppine.

cont.

SERVES 4

¾ cup [105 g] all-purpose flour

Kosher salt

Freshly ground black pepper

1½ lb [680 g] veal scaloppine, about 8 slices, patted dry with a paper towel

3 Tbsp neutral oil, such as canola or vegetable oil

1 Tbsp olive oil

12 oz [340 g] assorted mushrooms (my go-to mix are shiitake, cremini, and oyster), halved and tough stems trimmed off

cont.

In a large, shallow dish, whisk together the flour, 1 tsp salt, and several grinds of pepper. Set aside.

Dredge the veal slices in the seasoned flour to coat, shaking off the excess. (Really shake it over the bowl, otherwise excess flour will burn in the pan, making the sauce gloppy.) Transfer to a large plate or platter and set aside.

In a large skillet, preferably cast iron, over medium-high heat, add the neutral oil and warm until it shimmers. Add the veal slices in a single layer and cook, leaving them undisturbed, until their undersides are golden brown, about 2 minutes. Use a spatula to flip them over and transfer to a clean plate. Set aside.

To the same skillet, add the olive oil, mushrooms, and a generous sprinkle of kosher salt. Cook, stirring occasionally, until the mushrooms release their water and soften, 3 to 5 minutes (if you are using shiitakes, they take for*ever*).

Now, stop here and read this out loud: Pull the pan away from the stove when adding the Marsala because it may go up in flames. Are we all good? Continue.

Add the Marsala, butter, veal demi-glace, and parsley and squeeze that lemon wedge right into the skillet. Return the veal to the pan, uncooked-side down, and cook in the sauce until the sauce thickens, the underside browns, and the veal cooks through while soaking up all the flavors in the skillet, 1½ to 2 minutes.

Transfer this abbondanza to a serving platter, drizzle with extra-virgin olive oil, and sprinkle with Maldon sea salt flakes. Serve immediately.

½ cup [120 ml] dry Marsala wine (see headnote)

2 Tbsp butter

¼ cup [60 ml] store-bought veal demi-glace

2 Tbsp finely chopped fresh Italian parsley

1 lemon wedge

Extra-virgin olive oil, for drizzling

Maldon sea salt flakes

2 cups [480 ml] red wine,
preferably Spanish Rioja

3 Tbsp honey

1 orange, skin-on,
sliced into thin wheels
(use a very sharp knife!)

1 shallot, thinly sliced

3 garlic cloves, smashed

3 springs fresh thyme

¼ cup [60 ml] olive oil

1½ lb [680 g] skirt
steak, fat trimmed

Kosher salt

Freshly ground black pepper

2 Tbsp neutral oil

Maldon sea salt flakes

SANGRIA-MARINATED SKIRT STEAK

Selfishly enough, I love skirt steak because it cooks fast over high heat! And when you have limited grill space in a tiny restaurant like Little Owl, it's a perfect meat to cook up and send right out to a guest. Paired with a Little Gem Caesar with Panko Crunchies (page 78), it's a fast weeknight preparation for you, too! I also like skirt steak because it has a strong offal flavor (the cut is from the diaphragm muscle, placing it in close proximity to the liver) and it's a thin cut of meat, which means it takes on great flavor and tenderizes quickly in a marinade. Note: You will want to marinate the steak in the morning to use the same evening, but I wouldn't go longer than 12 hours, otherwise it will soften the steak too much, ruining the texture.

In a large glass mixing bowl (large enough to contain the sangria marinade and the steak), combine the wine, honey, orange wheels, shallot, garlic, thyme, and olive oil. Place the steak in the marinade, cover the top of the bowl tightly with plastic wrap, and refrigerate for a minimum of 6 hours and up to 12 hours.

Remove the steak from the marinade and season generously with salt and pepper on both sides. Set aside.

In a large cast-iron skillet over high heat, warm the neutral oil until it shimmers. Gently place the steak in the skillet and cook until the underside is browned (don't move it or touch it, just let it do its thing), about 2 minutes. Flip and cook until the other side is browned too, 1 to 2 minutes more, depending on the thickness of the steak. Transfer to a plate and let rest for 7 to 10 minutes before slicing it, otherwise you'll leak out all the juices that belong in the meat and on your plate!

Slice the steak against the grain, the same way you would slice a flank steak to prepare it for braciole (see "Let's Talk Meat for the Gravy," page 206). Transfer to a serving platter. Sprinkle the steak with Maldon sea salt flakes and more grinds of pepper, if you like. Serve alongside a Little Gem Caesar with Panko Crunchies (page 78).

LAMB T-BONES

SERVES 4

Eight 2 in [5 cm] thick
lamb loin "T-bone" chops

½ cup [120 ml] olive oil

¼ cup [60 ml] fresh
lemon juice

2 Tbsp Madras curry
powder

1 Tbsp Dijon mustard

2 Tbsp finely chopped
fresh rosemary

1 Tbsp sambal chili paste

2 Tbsp honey

2 garlic cloves, finely
chopped

Kosher salt

Freshly ground black pepper

More commonly referred to as lamb loin chop, a lamb T-bone contains
the loin and the tenderloin separated by a bone in the shape of a *T*. I think
Lamb T-Bone is a splashy name that evokes the remarkably rich flavor that
this cut of lamb offers for a fraction of the price of lamb chops. Purchase
2 in [5 cm] thick lamb T-bone cuts to take on the funky heat and flavor
of my delicious Madras curry marinade, which turns a beautiful saffron
color overnight. This deep and luscious big love dish pairs beautifully
with Potato Fontina Fonduta, and is also perfect to serve with a brightly
acidic Watercress Salad and Pickled Red Onion (page 84). Note: You
will marinate the lamb T-bones overnight and prepare the next day,
removing the lamb from your refrigerator to come to room temperature
1 hour before cooking.

Place the lamb in a large glass baking dish and set aside.

In a large mixing bowl, whisk together the olive oil, lemon juice,
curry powder, mustard, rosemary, chili paste, honey, and garlic
until well incorporated. Pour the marinade over the lamb, cover
with plastic wrap, and refrigerate for a minimum of 12 hours.

Preheat the oven to 400°F [200°C].

Remove the lamb from the marinade and blot off any excess oil with
a paper towel to avoid any fiery flare-ups in your skillet. Aggressively season all sides of the lamb (including the fat side—any salt
on that side will melt off while cooking) with salt and pepper.

Turn on your exhaust fan, as it may get a bit smoky.

In a large cast-iron skillet over high heat, place the lamb T-bones
fat-side down and cook until the fat gets crispy, about 1 minute.
Using tongs, carefully flip and grill on the other side until nicely
browned, about 2 minutes. Flip the lamb and repeat on the other
side, about 2 minutes more. Since there is honey in the marinade, don't leave them too long on each side, or the sugar will
begin to burn!

Turn and place the lamb bone-side down (it's called the chine
bone) so that the heat evenly distributes while they cook. Transfer
the cast-iron skillet to the oven and cook until the lamb is firm to
the touch, about 15 minutes. Transfer the lamb from the skillet
to the plate, bone-side down, to let rest for 5 to 10 minutes
before serving with Potato Fontina Fonduta (page 99).

CHAPTER 6

Fish and Seafood

🌿 Fish and Seafood

Even before my parents bought a house in Wildwood, New Jersey, I was lake fishing as a Boy Scout. My childhood fishing was pure instinct and full of great catches. Whatever I used—a red devil lure, a bobber, or a frog that I caught as bait—I caught a fish! The older I got, I accepted that there was more skill than luck involved. I stuck with it, I learned, I failed often (my motto became "Keep sucking till you succeed"), and I began to realize my fishing failures deepened the joy of my fishing successes. That feeling of catching a fish, bringing it home, cleaning it, sharing the story of my adventure, cooking it, serving it, and eating it with people I love became as natural as breathing.

My connectedness to my family, the water, and the mystery and beauty it offers (as well as the respect for sustainable fishing practices) began at a very early age. For those who know me well, they understand that my identity as a chef is intimately tied to my identity as a fisherman; they are both absolutely what I live for. When I am on the water, I stare out into the horizon, not a speck of land in sight, and trust that I know which way lies north. Making space to feel so vulnerable and alone on the water and working in tandem with nature is a powerful and beautiful feeling. It is a therapy for me. It is the same thing with cooking.

I know many of you will feel totally confident cooking fish at home, and my wish is that these recipes inspire you and bring some fresh ideas to your repertoire. For those of you who fear the vulnerability of a whole fish in your hands, take heart. I am here. Let me show you just what to do. North is this way.

Littleneck Clams *with Juicy Bread* 168

Crab Cakes *with Beefsteak Tomatoes* 172

Grilled Scallops
with Chicories, Bread Crumbs, and Anchovy Dressing 175

Halibut *with Basil Pesto, Sweet Corn, and Pea Salad* 177

Arctic Char
with Sugar Snap Peas, Radishes, and Avocado Crema 181

Summer Flounder Francese
with Zucchini and Yellow Squash 183

Whole Fish *with Olive Vinaigrette* 185

Horseradish-Crusted Cod
with Chive Mashed Potatoes and Lemon Crème Fraîche 189

Italian Fish Stew 193

CLEANING CLAMS I love clams so much that I opened a restaurant just blocks from Little Owl with my business partner, friend, and amazing chef Mike Price called The Clam. At The Clam, we celebrate one of nature's most perfect foods—a sustainable, low-fat, high-protein gift that tastes like the sea and the wind. Your littleneck clams will most likely come from a fishmonger or grocery store where they may already have the sand and grit removed from them. But, just to be sure, I want you to do this simple prep step before cooking them: Place the clams in a large, deep bowl and fill with very cold water until completely submerged. Add a handful of flour to the water—this forces the clams to purge themselves of any sand or impurities that might be inside them. Let sit for 30 minutes. Remove each clam one by one (any grit will have sunk to the bottom, so don't stir it up by draining them) and use a stiff brush to give each one a quick scrub under cold running water to be sure they are free of sand and grit.

LITTLENECK CLAMS
with Juicy Bread

SERVES 4 AS AN APPETIZER OR 2 AS A MAIN COURSE

Clams

4 lb [1.8 kg] littleneck clams, cleaned and removed of sand and grit (see note, above)

1 cup [220 g] butter, at room temperature

2 Tbsp finely chopped fresh Italian parsley

3 large garlic cloves, finely diced

1 Tbsp sambal chili paste

1 tsp celery salt

1 cup [240 ml] dry vermouth

1 lemon

For my fortieth birthday, I gathered some friends in Miami, opened lots of wine, cooked up some gorgeous littleneck clams, and served them with garlic-rubbed crusty bread to dip in the clam broth and soak up the juices. My dear old friend Gerad Argeros earnestly asked me, "Hey, Joe, what do you call this?" And "juicy bread" was born. Sometimes, you just gotta call a thing what it is. (It's good, so make a lot and serve it often!) For the record, littleneck clams, cherrystone clams, and topneck clams all belong to the same species of clam; they are just of varying sizes. And littleneck clams are the perfect size for a light meal or an appetizer. Save the larger cherrystones for their beautiful, natural clam broth, and serve them chopped up for my Spaghetti and Clams (page 107).

To prepare the clams: In a large, deep pot, combine the clams, butter, parsley, garlic, chili paste, celery salt, and vermouth. Using a fine grater (such as a Microplane), remove the zest from the lemon and add it to the pot. Cut the zested lemon in half, squeeze the juice into the pot, and cover. Turn the heat to high and cook until the clams fully open, about 10 minutes.

To prepare the juicy bread: Preheat your broiler.

Place the bread slices on a baking sheet and toast under the broiler for 1 minute. Turn and toast the other side for 1 minute more—watch it closely, they can burn fast! When the bread is cool enough to handle, use your hands to rub the peeled garlic cloves all over one side of the crusty bread. The texture of the bread grates the garlic until it disappears. Drizzle with olive oil and sprinkle with Maldon sea salt flakes.

Divide the clams among four bowls and top with slices of the bread. Serve immediately.

Juicy Bread

Twelve ½ in [12 mm] thick slices crusty baguette

2 whole garlic cloves, peeled

Extra-virgin olive oil, for drizzling

Maldon sea sat flakes

MY MOM'S TWO WAYS WITH CRAB

When my mom asks, "Hey, Joe, can you get me some crabs?" I'm on it! I don't know how many people can say this, but catching crabs for my mom is the best way I can show my love. I grab leftover chicken (there's always a leftover chicken somewhere in my life) or a fish carcass (ditto!) and call my buddy August Goulet, and we rent a boat to go handline crabbing for blue crabs down at the Jersey Shore. And I always come back with a bushel for her. But the part that really shows my big love for her is she makes me take the shell off and clean the guts! That's sacrilege to me! I love the guts and the layer of fat, called the "mustard"—it's the most flavorful part, but still, she makes me clean it. As a chef, this is hard. But as a son, I am all in. (By the way, she has no idea what I may have gone through to get those crabs—I often get bit, and then she wants me to wash all the flavor out?)

But I have to admit, she has a way with cooking crabs that I adore. Two ways, actually. And here they are: The first, in a large aluminum pan, lay down a dozen crabs, drizzle with olive oil, sprinkle with diced garlic, and season with Old Bay seasoning (or use my Seafood Spice Mix, page 173). Stick a nugget of butter right into the cavity of each of the crabs, place the pan on a very hot outdoor grill, and close the lid. Give it 30 minutes, and they are done. And delicious.

Now, second, we gotta talk about crab gravy. Prepare a large pot of Simple Marinara (page 106), add 1 cup [240 ml] of red wine, slowly drop in 6 fresh crabs, add a generous pinch of red pepper flakes, and simmer over low heat for at least 45 minutes. This marinara is now called Crab Gravy. My mom likes it over spaghetti with freshly grated pecorino (yes, cheese on crab gravy spaghetti. Just do it!) and a cold beer.

Handline Crabbing

I love catching crabs so much that I developed a technique for all of you aspiring handline crabbers out there: Make sure you are in shallow, brackish water and use two anchors (most people use one) and anchor the boat perpendicular to the current, creating six to eight lanes. Crabs scurry sideways and they have all those legs to hold on to the ocean floor when they don't want to move, but when they swim, they just float with the flow. One anchor provides two lanes, on either side of the boat. But if you have two anchors, positioned perpendicular, you can create six to eight lanes, which means you have a better chance of catching those crabs! Go get 'em!

A Loosey-Goosey Recipe
from a Guy Who Knows Crab Boils (Me!)

Take the biggest pot you can get your hands on and fill it with 3 in [7.5 cm] of water. Add peeled corncobs, potatoes, onions, halved whole garlic cloves (a bunch of them), and lemons (a couple of them), put it on your stove, put the lid on it, and bring it to a boil for a good 5 to 8 minutes. Now it's time to layer your live, large Jimmy crabs in, and with each stack of crabs you place in there, dump some Old Bay seasoning on them. Continue to stack crabs and dump Old Bay, stack crabs and dump Old Bay, all the way to the top of the pot. Cover with a lid and forget about them for 15 minutes.

Meanwhile, in a separate small saucepan, add a stick of butter, a couple of garlic cloves, and some more Old Bay and cook it until the butter melts and begins to boil and the garlic softens. When the top crab turns red, open a can of beer and pour it over the top, letting all that seasoning wash off the crabs and fall to the bottom of the pot. Take the crabs out and serve this one-pot crab boil off paper plates with the corn, potatoes, and roasted garlic and your Old Bay garlic butter on the side. I love to reveal the sweetest, largest lump of crabmeat (hint: It's behind the flipper fins in the back) and dip it in that seasoned butter for hours and hours until I pass out. *Have I said too much?*

Crab Cakes

2 Tbsp butter

¼ white onion,
finely diced

1 stalk celery, finely diced

½ red bell pepper,
finely diced

1 egg

2 Tbsp mayonnaise

1 Tbsp Dijon mustard

¼ tsp cayenne pepper

½ tsp celery seed

½ tsp celery salt

2 Tbsp finely chopped
fresh Italian parsley

½ tsp freshly ground
black pepper

1 tsp kosher salt

1 lemon

1 lb [454 g] jumbo
lump crabmeat

4 cups [240 g] panko
bread crumbs

¼ cup [60 ml] neutral oil,
such as canola or vegetable

Tomatoes

4 large, ripe beefsteak
tomatoes, cored and cut
into 8 wedges each

Maldon sea salt flakes

Freshly ground black pepper

6 fresh basil leaves,
roughly torn

Extra-virgin olive oil,
for drizzling

CRAB CAKES
with Beefsteak Tomatoes

I want you to make the best big love crab cakes that you can, and that means big, beautiful lumps of crab all throughout the cake. So here are my most important tips: Whenever possible, buy fresh jumbo lump crabmeat instead of pasteurized crabmeat. Even if the name on the label has an East Coast name, any pasteurized crabmeat is most likely preserved sweet blue crab from Thailand or Vietnam and you can definitely taste the difference. The best (and most expensive) is fresh jumbo lump crabmeat that will be sold at the fish counter.

Next, if you are investing in fresh crabmeat, you want to protect your investment and be as gentle with it as possible. To easily remove any tiny pieces of shell without having to pick through it, turn your broiler on high, spread out the fresh crabmeat on a baking sheet, and broil for 30 seconds. Any small, remaining shells will be revealed for easy picking. Biting into a shell in an otherwise perfectly prepared crab cake is so unpleasant—for you, and your guests (I am thinking of your reputation, here!).

And lastly, I want you to think about the technique of folding (similar to folding egg whites into a cake batter so they remain airy and fluffy) when you add the crab to the mix. Don't break it up or mash it in. And always make sure the last thing you add is the crab. You want these big love crab cakes full of jumbo love.

They make a wonderful summer dinner served alongside Roasted Corn, Spicy Mexican Style (page 89).

To make the crab cakes: In a medium pan over low heat, melt the butter and add the onion, celery, and bell pepper. Cook until soft, 4 to 5 minutes. Transfer to a small bowl and cool in the refrigerator for 25 to 30 minutes.

Meanwhile, in a large bowl, combine the egg, mayonnaise, mustard, cayenne pepper, celery seed, celery salt, parsley, black pepper, and kosher salt and whisk to incorporate. Using a fine grater (such as a Microplane), remove the zest from the lemon and add it to the bowl. Cut the zested lemon in half and squeeze the juice into the bowl. Add the crabmeat and use a rubber spatula (or a wide, wooden spoon) to gently fold the mixture together until just incorporated, being careful not to break up the crabmeat. You want to see the beautiful lumps of meat throughout your cakes!

Add the reserved vegetable mixture and 1 cup [60 g] of the bread crumbs to the crab mixture. Mix gently to incorporate. Once mixed, separate the mixture into 8 portions, right there in your bowl. The easiest way is to use your hands to cut through the mixture by dividing it in half, then dividing those halves into quarters and finally dividing those quarters into eighths. Boom. Eight crab cake portions.

Scatter the remaining 3 cups [180 g] of bread crumbs on a baking sheet and get ready to pack your cakes! Now, listen up: The secret to packing crab cakes is in the gentle pressure that you apply, while simultaneously turning the cake. This will keep it light yet well combined so that it holds together without crushing the crabmeat. Using your hands and working with one portion of the crab mixture at a time, place the crab mixture in the palm of your hand and lightly form it into a ball. Hold the ball in one hand like you are loosely gripping a cup. Using a circular motion, turn the ball in your hand, while using the opposite hand to apply gentle pressure to the top of the ball with your thumb. Pack it down as you turn, applying more pressure to all parts of the surface area, using your fingers to smooth the edges until it forms a cake. Gently dredge the top and bottom of the crab cake in the reserved bread crumbs, then roll it through the bread crumbs to coat the cake on all sides. Set aside. Repeat to make the remaining 7 cakes, until you have used up all of your crab mixture. Chill them in the refrigerator for 1 hour. This will firm them up for frying!

To prepare the tomatoes: Using a sharp knife, slice the tomatoes into thick slices and transfer to a large plate or platter. Sprinkle with Maldon sea salt flakes and several grinds of fresh pepper, scatter the torn basil leaves across the top, and finish with drizzles of olive oil. Set aside.

In a large skillet over medium-high heat, warm the neutral oil until it shimmers. Test it by dropping a few bread crumbs into the pan. Does it sizzle? Great, the oil is ready! Lower the heat to medium (to maintain the temperature in the pan), add the crab cakes, working in batches, if necessary, and cook until the undersides are golden brown (lift one gently with a spatula to take a peek), about 3 minutes. Carefully turn the crab cakes and cook until the second side is golden, too, another 2 to 3 minutes.

Transfer the crab cakes to a serving platter. Serve immediately, with the sliced beefsteak tomatoes.

YOU WANT MY SEAFOOD SPICE MIX?

I love Old Bay seasoning, but I often use my own spice mix for cooking crabs. You want it? You got it!

MAKES ¼ CUP

1 Tbsp garlic powder

1 Tbsp onion powder

1 Tbsp cumin

1 Tbsp celery salt

1½ tsp cayenne pepper

½ tsp ground cloves

2 or 3 dried bay leaves

Combine everything in a spice grinder or in the work bowl of your food processor and grind or pulse until it has the consistency of a fine seasoning. Store in an airtight container.

SCALLOP LOVE When you see the words *diver scallops*, it means someone actually dove off a boat, into the water, down to the bottom of the ocean to harvest the scallops by hand, then hauled them back up to a dayboat—a boat that legally has 1 day to go out fishing and then must return to port the same day. It's so much better than using a net and indiscriminately dragging the ocean floor and hurting the other creatures of the sea. Also, since these types of scallops are on the boat for only 1 day, they are not preserved in a chemical liquid brine to extend their shelf life. These other scallops, known as "wet scallops," will never taste as good as diver scallops. You can try rinsing them though, if you buy them. But chances are that they've soaked up and retained the preservative. For my scallop recipe, look for these key words: *U-10 diver scallops* (there will be 8 to 10 per lb [455 g]). If you find them, cook them the same day that you buy them, because like lots of beautiful things in life, they fade fast.

GRILLED SCALLOPS
with Chicories, Bread Crumbs, and Anchovy Dressing

Many chefs love to season dry dayboat scallops with just a little salt and pepper and let them sit undisturbed in a very hot skillet to get a great crusty brown caramel color on them. That's a wonderful way to enjoy them! However, when you marinate these scallops, they will quickly soak up the vivacious lemon herb flavor of the marinade. And a grill gives them a light smoky flavor that you can even achieve on an indoor griddle. If your scallops come with the connective muscle (called the foot) still attached, gently pull it from the scallop and discard. It's tough and you won't like it. In my part of the world, dayboat scallops come into peak, out of Maine, when the weather is at its worst, typically December through March. I look for hearty, cool-weather chicories, like radicchio and frisée (or even Belgian or curly endive) to provide a light bitterness. They turn tender once they wilt a bit from the warm Sherry Shallot Vinaigrette. Note: The best part about this dish is that once you prepare the scallops 1 hour ahead of time, the rest of the preparation comes together so fast!

cont.

SERVES 4 AS AN APPETIZER

1 garlic clove, smashed

1 fresh thyme sprig, de-stemmed and finely chopped

2 Tbsp olive oil

2 tsp minced lemon zest

1 lb [455 g] U-10 diver scallops, connective muscle removed from each (see headnote)

1 Tbsp butter

¾ cup [45 g] panko bread crumbs

¼ cup [60 ml] Sherry Shallot Vinaigrette (page 69)

cont.

2 fresh white Spanish boquerone anchovies (or in a pinch use 2 saltier, olive oil–packed anchovy fillets, drained)

2 Tbsp roughly chopped fresh Italian parsley

1 head radicchio (about 6 oz [170 g]), roughly torn

1 head frisée (about 6 oz [170 g]), roughly torn

Kosher salt

Freshly ground black pepper

Line a large plate with paper towels. Set aside.

In a large bowl, whisk together the garlic, thyme, olive oil and lemon zest. Add the scallops to the bowl and toss to coat with the marinade (little pieces of zest and thyme will stick to the scallops and they will look so beautiful!). Cover tightly with plastic wrap and place in the refrigerator for 1 hour.

In a large pan over medium heat, melt the butter. Add the panko bread crumbs and use a wooden spoon to stir constantly (so that they don't burn), or if you're feeling like a pro, lightly shake the pan back and forth so they alternate on and off the direct heat, cooking until golden, about 3 minutes. Transfer to the paper towel–lined plate to cool and set aside.

In a small pan over medium-low heat, combine the vinaigrette and the anchovies. Stir constantly (seriously, you don't want this to boil, or it will become bitter) until the anchovies melt—you can smash any lumps with your wooden spoon to help them along—about 1 minute.

Place the parsley, radicchio, and frisée in a large bowl and pour the warm vinaigrette over them. Use tongs to toss, allowing the warmth of the vinaigrette to wilt them a little bit, making a lovely salad base.

Preheat a cast-iron grill pan over medium-high heat for 5 minutes. Add a splash or two of neutral oil to a clean kitchen towel and rub it all over the grill pan to prevent the shellfish from sticking (if it smokes a little, turn on your exhaust fan!). Remove the scallops from the marinade and season generously with salt and grinds of pepper. Place the scallops on the grill and cook until the undersides are lightly browned and get a nice grill mark, about 1½ minutes. Rotate the scallops (don't flip them yet!) so you can make that very lovely crosshatch (be proud of it!) and cook an additional 30 seconds or so. Carefully flip the scallops and cook on the other side, until opaque and lightly browned, 1 to 2 minutes more.

Using your hands, divide the lettuces among four plates (twirling it around, placing little tufts in the center of the plate—it's a happy feeling!). Divide the grilled scallops around the salad tufts. Scatter the toasted bread crumbs on top of each dish. Serve immediately.

HALIBUT
with Basil Pesto, Sweet Corn, and Pea Salad

SERVES 4

I was in Spain the first time I saw mayonnaise slathered on fish. My former mother-in-law had covered a cod, head to tail, with an entire jar of Hellmann's and baked it. That whole cod, up to its eyeballs in browned mayonnaise, did something to me! Flash-forward to the early days of Little Owl. The former *New York Times* food critic Frank Bruni came for dinner on a terrifically busy night made more chaotic because my stove was on the fritz! I had only half of my burners working and, luckily, my salamander broiler, but I had a full-to-the-brim restaurant. Mr. Bruni ordered the halibut. It was supposed to be pan-seared over a sweet and tiny corn and pea salad—the first of the spring's bounty that year. But I didn't have any room on the stove to cook it! So, in a jolt of inspiration (panic? act of bold confidence?), I mixed some homemade pesto into aioli, slathered it on his fish, and stuck it under the broiler. Somewhere in me, the memory of my mother-in-law's mayonnaise fish seized me, and I captured the moment to make it my own. My sous chef Gustavo looked at me doubtfully and said, "You sure you want to do that?" And I am so glad that I did! The unforgettable creamy crust on the halibut was the most celebrated dish in his review. And it's become a Little Owl spring favorite on my menu ever since.

To make your life easier, you can simply bake this in the oven at 425°F [220°C] to achieve the same result. Note: The cook time truly depends on the thickness of your fillet, but a good test is to flake the fish with a fork—if it flakes easily, it is done. And here's a comforting thought: Don't worry about overcooking your fish; the basil pesto mayonnaise crust keeps the fish juicy. And if you use frozen peas or corn, just follow the cooking directions on the package.

3 ears fresh corn, in the husk, or 1 cup [140 g] frozen corn kernels

1 cup [150 g] fresh peas, shucked, or 1 cup [120 g] frozen peas

¼ cup plus 1 Tbsp [80 ml] Basil Pesto (page 125)

¼ cup [60 g] good store-bought mayonnaise

8 red grape tomatoes, halved

½ cup [30 g] snow pea sprouts

1 small handful frisée (or other fresh salad green, such as watercress or arugula)

8 thin slices red onion

2 Tbsp Sherry Shallot Vinaigrette (page 69)

Kosher salt

Freshly ground black pepper

Four 6 oz [170 g] center-cut skinless halibut fillets (or an alternate thicker-cut fish like swordfish or cod)

Preheat the oven to 425°F [220°C].

Place the ears of corn on the center rack of the oven and roast for 45 minutes. Remove and set aside to cool.

Prepare an ice water bath by filling a large bowl (preferably metal) with cold water and ice cubes. Set aside.

cont.

Meanwhile, in a large pot over high heat, bring 6 cups [1.4 L] of water to a boil. Add the fresh peas to the boiling water and cook until the peas float to the top, about 30 seconds. Continue to cook for about 1 minute longer; these little nuggets are hard and take some time. You'll know they're ready if you taste one—it should be tender yet firm and pop in your mouth. Use a large skimmer spoon to immediately transfer the peas to the ice water bath (this stops the cooking process and retains the peas' bright springtime-green color) and let cool for 1 minute. Drain in a colander and set aside. Want my two cents on this big-deal prep for these little peas? Springtime comes but once a year and fresh peas deserve your loving preparation. (I know you did right by them.)

In a small bowl, combine ¼ cup [60 ml] of the pesto and the mayonnaise and whisk thoroughly to combine. Set aside.

Peel the corn and remove the kernels from the cob by holding the cob upright on a cutting board and running the blade of a kitchen knife down the sides of each ear. Collect the kernels and place them in a medium bowl. Add the peas, tomatoes, pea sprouts, frisée, red onion, remaining 1 Tbsp of basil pesto, and the vinaigrette. Season with a pinch of salt and grinds of pepper and use tongs to toss well. Set aside.

Line a large baking sheet with aluminum foil and use your hands to rub 2 Tbsp of butter all over the foil so that the fish doesn't stick.

Place the halibut fillets about 2 in [5 cm] apart on the prepared baking sheet and generously season them with salt and pepper on both sides. Smear the basil pesto mayonnaise over the top of each fillet and cook until the basil pesto mayonnaise transforms into a creamy, melted crust with bubbly brown spots in some parts, 8 to 10 minutes.

Divide the corn and pea salad among four plates and set the halibut fillets on top. Serve immediately.

ARCTIC CHAR
with Sugar Snap Peas, Radishes, and Avocado Crema

Arctic char has a wonderful layer of fat to protect it from the very cold Arctic lakes that they swim in. And I love the smell of a fatty fish cooking (it reminds me of the smell of melted butter) because as that fat is melting, it's lending a rich, delicious flavor to the fish. What enchants me about this dish is the taste explosion of luscious hot char over a pool of cool, ethereal avocado crema (which is simply delicious homemade guacamole taken to new heights once you pass it through a fine-mesh sieve). Balance all that creamy love with gently cooked sugar snap peas for a refreshing crunch on your plate! And since I am obsessed with balancing textures in my dishes, cooking the fish skin-side down makes for a wonderful, crispy skin that imparts a lovely crackle in your bite. I'm coming to *your* house for dinner, if you make me this!

Note: If you like your char more on the medium-rare side, reduce the cooking time to 1 minute on the flipped side. Also, what do you do if the skin-side of a fish is stuck? Don't panic. Convince your fish that it is not stuck by gently grasping it with tongs and wiggling it a little, side to side, and saying "You're not stuck" in a kind tone. The skin will usually unstick from the bottom of your pan. Also, slide your slotted spatula as close as you can between the skin and the pan and lift up with confidence.

To make avocado crema: In a blender, add the avocado, jalapeño, onion, lime juice, cilantro, olive oil, and ½ tsp salt and blend until it becomes a very creamy guacamole, about 20 seconds.

Using a rubber spatula (so that you can scrape the sides and get every bit of guacamole out of the blender), transfer the guacamole to a fine-mesh sieve set over a small bowl. Push the guacamole through the sieve, really giving it some elbow grease, swirling it around and around until it all comes through the other side and into the bowl in an airy mound. Be sure to scrape the outer bottom of the sieve to scoop up any clingy guacamole remnants.

cont.

SERVES 4

Avocado Crema

2 ripe avocados, pitted

1 jalapeño pepper, ribs removed (and seeds, too, for less heat if desired) and finely diced

¼ white onion, diced

2 Tbsp fresh lime juice

2 Tbsp finely chopped fresh cilantro leaves

2 Tbsp extra-virgin olive oil

Kosher salt

Sugar Snap Peas

2 Tbsp neutral oil, such as vegetable or canola

1 Tbsp butter

8 oz [230 g] sugar snap peas, stem ends and strings removed

Kosher salt

Freshly ground black pepper

6 cherry tomatoes, halved

1 cup [20 g] fresh salad greens, such as watercress, frisée, or arugula, roughly chopped

2 radishes, ends trimmed and thinly sliced on a mandoline

2 Tbsp Sherry Shallot Vinaigrette (page 69)

Four 6 oz [170 g] arctic char fillets (salmon or trout fillets work great, too!)

Extra-virgin olive oil, for drizzling

To make the sugar snap peas: In a medium saucepan over low heat, warm the neutral oil until it shimmers, then add the butter and snap peas. Season generously with salt and a few grinds of pepper and cook, gently letting the butter melt and coat the beans, until the peas soften slightly but still retain a crisp crunch, 1 minute. Set aside.

Meanwhile, in a medium bowl, combine the tomatoes, greens, radishes, and vinaigrette. Add the warm snap peas and gently toss to combine. Set aside.

Preheat a cast-iron grill pan over medium-high heat for 5 minutes. Add a splash or two of neutral oil to a clean kitchen towel and rub it all over the grill pan to prevent the fish from sticking. Season the char fillets generously with salt and a few grinds of black pepper and place them on the grill, skin-side down, and grill until the skin gets crispy and the fish is almost cooked through, 2 to 3 minutes. Use a slotted spatula to flip the fish and continue grilling until cooked through, 2 to 3 minutes more, depending on the thickness of your fish.

Divide the avocado crema among four plates and top with the fish. Let it rain snap pea salad down on them, along with drizzles of extra-virgin olive oil. Serve immediately.

SUMMER FLOUNDER FRANCESE
with Zucchini and Yellow Squash

There is nothing French about this dish (even though the word *Francese* means "French" in Italian), but I also guarantee that you won't find Flounder Francese in Italy, either. As far as I know, it's as about Italian-American as you can get. And it's delicious! Instead of dredging the fish in egg and coating it with flour, as we do with with veal or chicken, here we reverse it. The egg goes on the outside, making a light, eggy crust that keeps the fish moist. I love to serve this with some zucchini and squash, and when I cook them, I treat them like I would a steak, cutting them into round coins and just cooking on one side in the pan. It keeps the vegetables from getting watery and mushy. The silky butter sauce that accompanies the vegetables and fish is spiked with my Simple Marinara (page 106) for a touch of bright color and a bit of acidity. (And I know this is a fish chapter but, yoo-hoo, you can make plain old thinly sliced chicken breasts come alive with this preparation, too!)

In a large shallow pan over high heat, warm 2 Tbsp [30 ml] of the oil until it shimmers. Add the squash and zucchini, season generously with salt and pepper, and cook, undisturbed, until the underside of the squash and zucchini turn brown and soften slightly (you want them to retain texture and have a bite), about 2 minutes. Add the olives, capers, garlic, ½ of the white wine, the marinara, 1 tsp of the lemon juice, and 1 Tbsp of the butter. Cook until the liquid reduces a bit, 3 to 4 minutes. Turn the squash and zucchini over, giving it all a stir, and remove from the heat. Transfer to a large, pretty serving platter and set aside.

In a small dish, add the flour. Crack the eggs into a medium bowl and lightly beat them. Set aside.

Season the fish fillets generously on both sides with salt and pepper. One at a time, dredge them lightly in the flour, shaking off the excess back into the dish, and then submerge the flour-coated fillet in the beaten egg. After this dredge-and-swim routine, set the fish aside.

cont.

SERVES 4

4 Tbsp [60 ml] neutral oil

1 large yellow squash, ends trimmed, cut into ½ in [12 mm] thick coins

1 large zucchini, ends trimmed, cut into ½ in [12 mm] thick coins

Kosher salt

Freshly ground black pepper

12 black olives, pitted

1 Tbsp capers

1 garlic clove, thinly sliced

1 cup [240 ml] dry white wine, preferably Chablis or Sauvignon Blanc

¼ cup [60 ml] Simple Marinara (page 106) or store-bought marinara

1 tsp fresh lemon juice (or squeeze 1 wedge), plus ½ cup [120 ml] fresh lemon juice

3 Tbsp butter

½ cup [70 g] all-purpose flour

2 eggs

Four 6 oz [170 g] flounder fillets, patted dry with a paper towel, or another flat fish like lemon sole or turbot

2 Tbsp finely chopped fresh Italian parsley leaves

In a skillet over medium-high heat, add the remaining 2 Tbsp [30 ml] of oil and warm until it shimmers. Place the flounder fillets in the pan and cook until the underside turns golden, about 1 minute. Carefully turn and cook the other side until golden, 1 minute more. To the pan, add the remaining ½ cup [120 ml] of white wine, ½ cup [120 ml] of lemon juice, and 2 Tbsp of butter, and 1 Tbsp of the chopped parsley, and continue cooking until the butter melts and the fish absorbs all the flavors and cooks through, about 2 minutes more. Use a slotted spatula to transfer the fish, reserving the Francese sauce in the skillet, and place the fillets over the zucchini and squash.

Raise the heat to high and cook the reserved sauce until it reduces a bit and comes to a boil. As soon as it begins to boil, remove it from the heat and pour it over the fish.

E voila! Eccola! Here it is! Family-style Flounder Francese! Sprinkle with the remaining 1 Tbsp of fresh chopped Italian parsley leaves and serve immediately.

FISH FEAR Tell me the truth: Has the fear of bones, fins, eyeballs, and faces stopped you from cooking a whole fish at home? If so, I invite you to work through your fish issues with me. One time I had to cook sardines for a famous actor and he ate everything. *Every. Thing.* I don't like the way eyeballs taste, but he loved them—even *I* had an issue with that one! But, I want you to know that by cooking a fish whole (with head and skeleton intact), you can make a deeply flavored fish with a moist and succulent texture. And the presentation is simply beautiful. And that, my friend, is an opportunity to earn some big confidence in the kitchen. So, let's embrace it with a simple, confidence-boosting recipe, shall we?

WHOLE FISH
with Olive Vinaigrette

The most important thing when preparing whole fish is to source your fish at a grocery store that has a reputation for expertly handling fresh fish. Or if you have a fish market in your hometown, go there! (In New York, if I am not cooking my own catch, I go to Citarella or the Lobster Place in Chelsea Market.) Rest assured that the messy work is already done for you—any fish that is on display has already been eviscerated, meaning that anything that would make that fish highly perishable (stomach and guts) has been removed. It has also been bled and scaled. But, if you see a fish with fins or gills left on it, just ask the person at the counter to remove them. And if you really can't bear the sight of eyeballs, yes, indeed you can ask them to remove the head. It will still taste delicious. You can use this recipe for any whole fish that you love, including porgy (*orata* in Italian or *dorade* in French), black sea bass, or red snapper. Most whole fish are in the 1¼ to 1½ lb [570 to 680 g] range, which includes the weight of the head and skeleton, so one fish per person is a perfect amount.

Preheat the oven to 375°F [190°C]. Line a large baking sheet with parchment paper and use your hands to rub 2 Tbsp of butter all over the parchment so that the fish doesn't stick. Set aside.

In a blender, add the basil, parsley, olives, anchovies, the juice of the reserved lemon half, ¼ cup [60 ml] olive oil, the sherry vinegar, a pinch of salt, and a few grinds of pepper and blend until awesome (and smooth), about 20 seconds. Set aside.

cont.

SERVES 4

6 fresh basil leaves

2 Tbsp finely chopped fresh Italian parsley leaves

¼ cup [40 g] kalamata olives, pitted

2 fresh white Spanish boquerone anchovies (or in a pinch, use 4 saltier, olive oil–packed anchovy fillets, drained)

1 large lemon, halved (reserve half and slice the other half into thin rings)

¼ cup [60 ml] olive oil, plus more for drizzling

2 Tbsp sherry vinegar

Kosher salt

Freshly ground black pepper

Four 1¼ to 1½ lb [570 to 680 g] whole fish, scaled, gutted, and cleaned (see headnote)

4 garlic cloves, smashed

2 small white onions, ends trimmed, peeled, and thinly sliced

4 sprigs fresh thyme

Place the fish on the baking sheet and generously season the cavity of each one with salt and pepper. Stuff each cavity with some lemon slices, a garlic clove, some onion slices, and a sprig of thyme. Drizzle the outside of each with olive oil and generously season the skin with salt and pepper.

Place in the oven and cook until the skin is crispy and the flesh underneath the thickest part of the fish (near the head) easily flakes when you poke it with a fork, 15 to 18 minutes, depending on the size of your fish. (And because I know some of you out there went ahead and had the head removed, please note that then the cook time could be as little as 13 minutes. Just saying.)

Transfer the fish to a beautiful serving platter and spoon over the olive vinaigrette. Serve immediately.

SALSA FRESCA

MAKES ABOUT 1 CUP [240 ML]

1 medium tomato, diced

½ medium red onion, diced

1 jalapeño pepper, ribs removed (and seeds, too, for less heat, if desired) and diced

½ large cucumber, seeded and diced (you can leave the skin on)

2 Tbsp finely chopped fresh basil leaves (or cilantro if preferred)

¼ cup [60 ml] extra-virgin olive oil

2 Tbsp fresh lemon juice

1 Tbsp kosher salt

Freshly ground black pepper

4 oz [115 g] cooked shrimp, chopped (optional)

4 oz [115 g] cooked lobster meat (optional)

4 oz [115 g] jumbo lump crabmeat (optional)

In a large bowl, combine the tomato, onion, jalapeño, cucumber, basil leaves, olive oil, lemon juice, salt, and several grinds of pepper and mix well with a wooden spoon until combined. If using shrimp, lobster, or crabmeat, add it last and give it another stir. Store in the refrigerator in an airtight container for up to 2 days.

A KISS OF PIZZAZZ ON YOUR FISH I love to top a simple piece of grilled fish or oven-roasted whole fish with a variety of fresh salsas or a quick pepper-fennel relish. They add a flavor component that is refreshing and bright right on top of whatever your catch is. Cooking the fennel makes it sweet and soft, and store-bought roasted peppers save you time! All these variations are delicious on top of Juicy Bread (see page 168) for a scrumptious bruschetta.

PEPPER-FENNEL RELISH

MAKES ABOUT 1 CUP [240 ML]

1 Tbsp neutral oil

½ small fennel bulb, trimmed and halved lengthwise and finely diced

Kosher salt

2 jarred, roasted red peppers, finely diced

2 fresh white Spanish boquerone anchovies (or in a pinch, use 2 saltier, olive oil–packed anchovy fillets, drained), roughly chopped

10 capers, rinsed and drained

1 tsp fresh lemon juice

3 Tbsp olive oil

1 Tbsp finely chopped fresh basil leaves

In a medium pan, add the oil, fennel, and a generous pinch of salt and then turn the heat to medium-high and cook, undisturbed, until the fennel gets very brown, about 2½ minutes. Using a wooden spoon, begin to stir continuously, until the fennel is browned all over and becomes soft and fragrant (little pieces may stick to the pan—it's OK), 3 to 4 more minutes. This process is similar to caramelizing onions (see "The Ugly Part," page 61), so the fennel will look a little ugly but will taste great in the relish! Remove from the heat and set aside.

In a medium bowl, combine the peppers, anchovies, capers, lemon juice, olive oil, and basil. Add the fennel and mix well with a wooden spoon until combined.

Serve as you wish! Transfer to an airtight container and store in your refrigerator for up to 4 days.

HORSERADISH-CRUSTED COD
with Chive Mashed Potatoes and Lemon Crème Fraîche

I began making this dish years ago when I was cooking in Los Angeles. And it was a favorite among my catering guests. The smell of the crusty, fresh horseradish topping combines with the delicate onion aroma of the chive mashed potatoes and a delectable crème fraîche sauce to evoke a favorite childhood comfort food: a bag of sour cream and onion potato chips. Your whole house will smell great when you cook it! Use a food mill or ricer to achieve fluffy, creamy mashed potatoes. Also note, when topping the fish with the bread crumb mixture, don't feel obligated to pile every last crumb on there. You will make a generous amount of horseradish mixture, so use it all if you like, or use less. I always think that it's better to have it and not need it, then need it and not have it. Any extra can be toasted in a pan for use on a salad the next day.

To make the chive mashed potatoes: Place the potatoes in a large pot, season generously with salt, and cover with cold water by at least 1 in [2.5 cm]. Cover and bring to a boil over medium-high heat, remove the lid, lower the heat to a simmer, and cook until the potatoes are fork tender but still offer a bit of resistance (you don't want them falling apart), about 12 minutes.

Meanwhile, in a blender, combine the chives and olive oil and blend to make a smooth purée, about 20 seconds. Set aside.

Drain the potatoes in a colander. Set a ricer (or food mill) over the now-empty potato pot and rice the potatoes, so that they fall in a fluffy mound back into the pot.

cont.

Chive Mashed Potatoes

2 lb [910 g] Idaho potatoes, peeled and quartered

Kosher salt

½ cup [25 g] roughly chopped chives, plus more for garnish if desired

⅔ cup [160 ml] extra-virgin olive oil

1 cup [240 ml] half-and-half

3 Tbsp butter

Freshly ground black pepper

3 Tbsp whole milk (if reheating the potatoes), plus more as needed

Topping for Fish

1 small horseradish root, peeled and roughly chopped (its odor is strong and will clear your airways!)

2 Tbsp butter

1 cup [60 g] panko bread crumbs

2 tsp kosher salt

2 Tbsp finely chopped fresh Italian parsley leaves

Four 6 oz [170 g] cod fillets

Freshly ground black pepper

Lemon Crème Fraîche Sauce

¼ cup [60 g] crème fraîche

¼ cup [60 ml] store-bought veal demi-glace

2 Tbsp fresh lemon juice

In a small saucepan over medium-low heat, combine the half-and-half and butter and slowly heat until the butter is melted. Add the mixture to the pot of riced potatoes and gently fold it in, using a rubber spatula (or the back of a wooden spoon) so that the potatoes absorb it all and get good and creamy. Taste for seasoning and add more salt and pepper. Add the chive purée and mix well to achieve uniform fresh, bright green colorful specks throughout the mashed potatoes. Cover to keep warm and set aside.

Preheat the oven to 425°F [220°C].

To make the cod: In a blender, combine the horseradish, butter, bread crumbs, salt, and parsley and blend for 10 seconds until it is well combined and finely crumbled. If it needs an extra pulse or two, go for it. Set aside.

Line a baking sheet with aluminum foil and rub it with 2 Tbsp butter to prevent the fish from sticking. Place the cod on the baking sheet, generously season with salt and a few grinds of pepper, and top with the horseradish mixture, patting it down so that it sticks and makes a crust. Bake until the horseradish topping is golden brown and the fish is opaque and flakes nicely when you poke it with a fork, 7 to 8 minutes, depending on the thickness of your fillet.

Meanwhile, prepare the lemon crème fraîche sauce: In a small saucepan over medium-low heat, add the crème fraîche, demi-glace, and lemon juice and whisk to combine. As soon as it comes to a boil, cover and set aside.

If you made the potatoes ahead of time, you can reheat them in a saucepan over low heat, adding 3 Tbsp of whole milk (or more), as needed, to help thin them out until they are heated through. Or not. (Sometimes they need it and sometimes they don't, especially if they are perfectly creamy; I trust you to make that call.)

Divide the chive mashed potatoes among four plates, top with generous spoons of sauce, place the cod fillet on top, and while you're add it, snip some more fresh chives for a nice touch! Serve immediately.

ITALIAN FISH STEW

The flavors in the marinara sauce combine with the natural, briny juices that get released by the seafood to make a quick fish stew that requires nothing else but some freshly chopped parsley. Don't overthink it or fret. Just get the best, freshest seafood you can buy and watch this one-pot seafood love unfold.

In a large pot over medium-high heat, place the seafood in the following order: clams on the bottom, followed by mussels, calamari, and shrimp. Top with the marinara and add the butter and basil. Cover with a lid and cook until the clams open, 10 to 12 minutes.

Divide among four bowls, sprinkle with sea salt, drizzle with olive oil, and serve immediately. (You're making Juicy Bread—see page 168—with this, right?)

SERVES 4 AS A MAIN COURSE

1 lb [455 g] littleneck clams (see note on cleaning clams, page 168)

1 lb [455 g] mussels, cleaned and debearded (it looks like a string hanging out of the shell; use your fingers to grasp and pull it downward toward the hinge of the shell)

1 lb [455 g] calamari, cleaned and cut into rings

1 lb [455 g] 16/20 shrimp, cleaned and unpeeled

4 cups [960 ml] Simple Marinara (page 106)

½ cup [110 g] unsalted butter

2 Tbsp finely chopped fresh basil leaves

Maldon sea salt

Extra-virgin olive oil

CHAPTER

7

Sunday Supper

Sunday Supper

In my family, and across Italian-American families in my neighborhood, Sunday supper is a cherished ritual of eating and connecting with each other around the table. And it's deepened by the effort and investment of time in cooking dishes with respect to shared history and tradition. In my house, Sunday supper was the love we shared for each other made manifest in food. And at the heart of each meal was a large pot of Sunday Gravy (page 211) filled with the luxurious comfort of my mom-mom's meatballs and cuts of meat, each lending dimension and depth, bubbling in a rich tomato base. Learning how to make a great Sunday gravy is essential to understanding that great cooking is about building layers of flavor: searing the meat before it goes into the liquid and allowing the sauce to reduce (scraping the ring that settles along the side of the pot, right back into the gravy), just two techniques that allow for more complex and dynamic taste. Make an entire pot of gravy with an arms-wide-open love to the folks whom you hold near and dear.

Or try my Little Owl Gravy Meatball Sliders (page 226) at home for the first time. These dishes are yours to savor as you wish. Each one will sing. Mortadella-Stuffed Cherry Peppers (page 234)—the easy appetizer that signaled the start of our Sunday feasting—are flavor-packed and ready to pop in your mouth. My mom-mom's "Homemades," toothsome homemade pasta noodles that soak up a rich gravy (page 221), can be made any day of the week. These recipes and others are woven together in this chapter like threads in a tapestry. The picture they create reaches for the layers and flavors of my South Philly upbringing on Queen Street. They tell the story of a time when I could *taste* big love, one block at a time, one Sunday at a time.

BACK TO QUEEN STREET

My house on the 500 block of Queen Street was between Catharine (with an *a* for the queen of Sweden—the Swedes built Penn's Landing and it used to be full of tiny buildings for long-ago people who were tiny, too) and Christian Streets.

Go up Christian Street and you run right into the Catholic school and the Bella Vista neighborhood. The parking lot for the school was our playground. And the little wooded area behind it was the worst place you can imagine kids to play—broken glass, discarded household items, weeds up to your hips.

A mess.

That's exactly where we went and played.

My South Philly childhood is frozen in any number of pictures of a bunch of us kids on a neighborhood front stoop; we're Italian, Black, Puerto Rican, Jewish; we're big brothers with arms around little sisters; we're little brothers in tube socks—is that Freddy Podogrosi? We're swigging soda and we're smiling with bright eyes straight at the camera while somebody's mom/aunt/grandmother clicks the shutter.

There's the House of Industry: a run-down building turned neighborhood kids' club, and on their roof you could find all the balls we'd play with.

One day, my brother Michael and I had an idea:

"Let's go on the roof and get all our balls."

While climbing the fire escape on our way up the side of the building a piece breaks off.

And

I'm about to fall to my death

And

My brother catches me in midair while I am on my way down, down, down.

How?

He must have gotten me by the pants.

And

We talk about it all the time.

There's John's Water Ice—the f-ing best. (They had only four flavors!)

Guerrera's butcher shop was on Eighth and Catharine. And

over there, on Seventh and Fulton, is the house my father grew up in (and where Gigi the monkey lived, too!).

And travel farther up to Eighth Street and you're entering the Italian Market. By the time you hit Ninth Street, BANG! It's all right here.

Sarcone's Bakery.

Ralph's, "the oldest Italian restaurant."

Ding Ho, where lo mein reminded us of spaghetti.

Palumbo's-CR Room (celebrity room) and The Nostalgia Room.

Let's take a moment of silence for Palumbo's (it burnt down, twice!).

You see, growing up, Palumbo's was the big thing if we ever went out to eat—and we hardly ever did, with food so good at home. And Frank Palumbo was a big deal.

He didn't just have a restaurant, he ran a hostel for Italian immigrants who needed to get

200   BIG LOVE COOKING

on their feet, and then he'd set them up with city jobs.

City of Brotherly Love kinda way.

I carry that with me in some way, I think. The things Frank Palumbo did for people.

Farther down, there is St. Mary Magdalen de Pazzi (the first Italian national parish in the United States) on narrow Montrose Street. Imagine my entire neighborhood lining up to get into church every Sunday or for the May Procession of Saints. Jammed.

In a New York kinda way.

The church is closed now, but they reopened it for my father's funeral . . .

Montrose Street reminds me so much of the West Village. All these little streets; you learn how to drive a car in the '70s and '80s in South Philly, you can drive anywhere.

Turn a bit and hit:

The Friendly Lounge (a bar).

Napoli Pizza (uh . . . pizza).

And Schmockey's (it was never spelled, so I can't guarantee that's right).

But the bartender, Frankie E., made a younger me feel so very proud to bring some older friends there when he left us a bottle on the bar to drink on the honor system.

The first thing out of his mouth when he saw me was, "Ain't you Compi's kid?"

After church, go to Ninth Street and head over to Di Bruno Bros. to get the cheese.

And there's Villa di Roma . . .

And Dante & Luigi's . . .

So many places steeped in old-world Italian-American traditions.

But for all the tradition, my mother was progressive (in a '70s sort of way), and so while all the other kids were sent to Catholic school, she chose to send us to McCall public school. Morning walks down Seventh to school were always met with a lift from anybody with a cool mode of transport: horses, hearses, and fire trucks.

But, taking South Sixth Street on the walk home was the best route for someone to pick you up and bring you back to Queen Street.

We're around the corner from my house now (and it's so much like the West Village—look how narrow Kauffman Street is!). And here it comes into sight:

My house.

My window.

My mom-mom, two doors down.

That over there is a cherry tree. And the Podogrosi's house—Freddy was just one of fourteen.

On my block was my uncle's house, a mix of families from all walks of life, and a vacant house. And somewhere in

between was the lady who had a hole in her face who everyone thought was a witch because she constantly yelled at us kids.

My row house had concrete steps.

But, if you had marble steps, you'd better have taken out your Ajax and a scrubby brush to keep them spic-and-span. We cared about each other and how clean you kept your steps.

Sometimes, now when I see South Philly, I don't even recognize where I am.

"This was the gas station."

"This was Goldstein's."

"There was an abandoned house here where we'd go and do 'whatever.'"

They're all developed now.

The only thing that remains is the pride of it once belonging to me.

LET'S TALK MEAT FOR THE GRAVY

Pull up a chair. I need to talk to you about the meats for the gravy.

When it comes to selecting what meats make a great gravy, I have to tell you that it's personal. What my grand-mom and mom may have chosen to put in our gravy on any given Sunday probably differed from what another family down the block chose to use. There were lots of Sundays when my grand-mom didn't add a pig's foot and the gravy was delicious. I person-ally have made Sunday gravy using only beef short rib, and it was dynamite. But this recipe is my most nostalgic South Philly Sunday gravy: When the stars were aligned and my grand-mom was at the stove, this is what we would have.

And because gravy is a meal in itself (and not a pasta topping), I've included a variety so you have a greater selection to choose from at the table. People love options. How many times have I heard "Oh! I love flank steak!" or "Oh, pass me a little bite of sausage!" while I watch them skip a meatball entirely (what!?). Also, each meat I have selected offers something different: Some impart a wonderful pork flavor, like fennel sausage and pork ribs, and others take on richness when cooked in liquid low and slow, like flank steak. And the balance of meats in the meat-ball recipe creates a perfect ratio of fat, which translates to flavor. And a pig's foot takes the gravy to another level, by adding some succulent natural gelatin. But if you're anything like me, and you thrive on necessity being the mother of invention, you can use your passion for or the availability of another cut of meat and still make a wonderful gravy. If a pig's foot doesn't make it into your gravy, or if you want to swap out beef short rib for flank steak, just know that you will not fail. Quite the opposite; you'll have captured the essence of big love cooking—making the gravy all yours.

First, the meatballs.

My grandmother's recipe uses a blend of ground beef, pork, and veal. And they are the same meatballs that I make for my Gravy Meatball Sliders (page 226) at Little Owl. Her secret ingredient? Cold water. When you add it to the meatball mix right before mixing, it adds necessary moisture to keep the meatballs juicy. Learning to cook with someone who grew up during the Great Depression, I noticed quickly that water was an important ingredient in many of her dishes. One difference in my meatballs versus my grand-mom's is that I use panko bread crumbs in my meatballs, because I like the texture. I don't really follow the rules for Italian cooking; I just use them as a guide and make them my own. Mix and chill your meatballs for at least 15 minutes in your refrigerator before browning. This gives the fat in the meatball time to congeal so that they will hold together in a tight, light ball. Or, you can also make them a day ahead and keep them in the refrigerator in an airtight container for the next day (even better). In the true spirit of abbondanza, you'll make more than you need, so you'll have plenty for leftovers. Pair them with homemade Gravy Meatball Slider Buns (page 225) and have a leftover gravy meatball slider feast. Or stick a fork in the fridge at 10 p.m. for a cold meatball snack, which is my favorite way to devour them. When it comes to meatballs, I surround myself with them. I think it's my way of keeping my family close to me.

Prepare braciole.

Slices of thinly pounded flank steak are layered with a slice of salami, pepperoni, or cheese, then bound together in a little bundle held together by string or a toothpick—you can purchase one piece of flank steak and slice and pound it at home. Since flank steak has a grain that runs from one end of the meat to the other, you want to cut the steak thinly, against that grain, so that you can achieve tender slices. Place the steak horizontally on a clean surface. Using a sharp boning knife, and using one hand on top as a guide, hold your knife at a 45-degree angle, perpendicular to the steak, and cut about 10 diagonal slices. Cutting the steak at an angle will give your slices more surface area so that you can create a nice wide escalope (a fancy way to say "thin slice of meat") to season and layer (or stuff). Lay plastic wrap across the steak pieces and pound each piece to ½ in [12 mm] thick using the flat side of a meat mallet. Or roll a wooden rolling pin or an unopened wine bottle over it (my favorite). If you ask your butcher to prepare it, just make sure you ask him or her to prepare slices cut against the grain and pounded so that you can stuff and roll them for small braciole. One really simple, old-school way of adding more depth of flavor to the braciole without overpowering it is to layer a slice of salami, soppressata, or pepperoni in the meat before rolling it up. You can even use prosciutto, chopped hard-boiled egg, and chunks of hard cheese to make it yours.

Italian sweet sausage with fennel seeds is a must.

Fiorella's Sausage supplied everyone in South Philly with theirs. The fragrant fennel makes the flavor of this Sunday gravy distinctly my grandmother's. And I love to add an extra teaspoon. The story goes, one Sunday morning, my grandmother couldn't pick up fennel sausage for the gravy, so she added fennel seeds directly to the gravy pot.

And please use country pork ribs.

They are meatier and less fatty than baby back ribs because they aren't ribs. Surprise! They are a cut of pork that is close to the shoulder blade. And they are perfect for low and slow cooking.

Now, on to the pig's foot.

On special occasions, a pig's foot would be added to our Sunday gravy. I don't know anyone who makes Sunday gravy with a pig's foot anymore, so if you toss it in, it's sure to make it unique! And the gooey, gelatinous, awesome-tasting pork is dynamite. Most grocery store pig's feet are sold cut in halves or quarters, already cleaned and debristled. You don't need to do anything with it except add it to the gravy. When you pull it out of the pot, if you don't want to put it on display on the table, that is fine, as some people think a pig's foot is creepy. Save it for yourself. Or save it for your kid or their cousins that peek in on you while you're cooking. Let them pick off of it. They might squeal "yuck! ewww!" at first, but once that piece of pig's foot goes into their mouth, they'll come to their senses—that's what happened to me!

I love talking with you.
So, let's begin.

SUNDAY GRAVY

This beautiful Sunday gravy is my North Star of big love cooking. Inspired by my grandmother's technique and my mother's interpretation, browning the meats first is one of the secrets (among others) to building rich, deep flavor. Sending the meat into the tomato liquid already flavor-packed will guarantee that it's mingling all of its complex meaty flavors with the tomato base as it simmers for hours on your stove. Now that I have your attention, see "Let's Talk Meat for the Gravy" (page 206). In my little row house in Queen Village, Sunday gravy was typically made on Saturday morning by my mom or grand-mom. If per chance someone got it in their head to make a weekday gravy and you woke up to the smell of browning meat at 7 a.m., it was a mad dash to the kitchen to see who else could possibly be at the stove, because, let's face it, some people make Sunday gravy better than others. And I want you to be one of those people. It is fine to make this gravy the day you will serve it, as long as you allow enough time for it to concentrate, which should be at least 4 hours.

Take out two large baking sheets (no need to oil them, they're there to hold the meats) and set them close by. Also, take out a large platter to hold the browned meats.

To prepare the meatballs: In a large bowl, combine the beef, pork, veal, eggs, 1 cup [240 ml] of cold water, the pecorino, bread crumbs, salt, pepper, and parsley. Use your hands to mix well and form tightly into 36 golf ball–size meatballs, about 3 oz [85 g] each. Cup your hands and roll them back and forth to really smooth them out and transfer to a baking sheet. Cover with plastic wrap and place them in the refrigerator to chill for at least 15 minutes while you carry on with the rest of the meats.

To prepare the braciole: Place the pounded pieces of flank steak on a clean work surface and season them generously on both sides with sprinkles of the fresh parsley and the salt and pepper. Lay a slice of cured meat on top of each steak. For each piece, starting at one end, roll up the steak tightly like a jelly roll and secure it with a toothpick. These fat little flank steak rolls are officially braciole. Transfer to the second baking sheet and set aside.

cont.

Meatballs

1 lb [455 g] ground beef

1 lb [455 g] ground pork

1 lb [455 g] ground veal

3 eggs

1 cup [60 g] finely grated pecorino cheese

1 cup [140 g] panko bread crumbs

Kosher salt

Freshly ground black pepper

¼ cup finely chopped fresh Italian parsley

Braciole

1 lb [455 g] flank steak, thinly sliced and pounded into about 10 slices (see "Let's Talk Meat for the Gravy," page 206)

1 Tbsp finely chopped fresh Italian parsley leaves

2 tsp kosher salt

½ tsp freshly ground black pepper

4 oz [115 g] thinly sliced cured meat (salami, soppressata, or pepperoni)

Gravy

1 lb [455 g] country-style pork ribs

Kosher salt

cont.

Freshly ground black pepper

1 cup [240 ml] canola oil

1 lb [455 g] sweet Italian sausage

¼ cup [60 ml] olive oil

1 large yellow onion, ends trimmed, peeled, and roughly sliced

8 garlic cloves, smashed

1 tsp fennel seed

½ cup [20 g] finely chopped fresh parsley

8 fresh basil leaves, finely chopped

½ tsp red pepper flakes (optional)

Four 28 oz [794 g] cans whole, peeled tomatoes

One 6 oz [170 g] can tomato paste

1 lb [455 g] pig's foot, cleaned and debristled

To make the gravy: Lay the pork ribs on a clean work surface and season them generously on both sides with salt and pepper. Transfer to the baking sheet with the braciole. The meatballs will most likely still need time to chill, so just be you and do something else. You will be browning each meat one at a time, making sure to hit all sides so that the color is dark and uniform. Commence the browning when the meatballs say they are ready.

In anticipation of browning the meat, I want you to know this: If a piece of sausage is holding on for dear life, if a bit of pig's foot puts its foot down and takes a stand on the bottom of your pot, just know that whatever you can't scrape off is going to flavor your gravy anyway. So, stay calm. You're in charge. Let's brown.

In the largest shallow pot you own (the one with the maximum amount of surface area so that you can comfortably brown the meats—even a large cast-iron skillet will work) over medium-high heat, add the canola oil. You want to get the oil very hot but not smoking. Remove the meatballs from the refrigerator and use a large slotted spoon to add one to the pot. Does that meatball immediately start to crisp on the outside? Good. Your oil is hot enough. Continue adding the rest of the meatballs to the pot, allowing ample space between each meatball and working in batches. Lower the heat to medium and cook them until they are dark brown and crusty on one side, 4 to 5 minutes. Turn and cook on the other side until that is brown and crusty, too, 4 to 5 minutes more. Persuade any stubborn meatballs that want to stick to the bottom of the pot by sticking a slotted spoon under them and giving a gentle shove. Transfer the meatballs to the large platter and set aside.

Using tongs, add the braciole to the pot and cook until brown and crusty all over, about 5 minutes. You'll have to roll these around a little bit since the toothpick is in the way; just get it uniformly dark and crusty. Transfer to the platter and set aside. Add the pork ribs and sausage to the pot and let them sit on one side and cook until dark brown, about 3 minutes. Turn and cook for 2 to 3 minutes more. Transfer to the platter and set aside.

Discard the canola oil by pouring it into a fine-mesh strainer placed over an empty can. The strainer will catch any brown bits of meat and the oil will cool in the can before you dump it—my grandmother and my mother would save a tomato can from their previous pot of gravy. Use whatever can or vessel is best for you. Set aside the strainer of meat bits.

In the same empty pot over medium-high heat, warm the olive oil until it shimmers and add the browned meat bits, onion, garlic, fennel seed, 2 Tbsp kosher salt, the parsley, and basil, lower the heat to medium, and cook until the onions are slightly brown and everything smells amazing, about 5 minutes. If you like your gravy spicy, now would be the time to add the red pepper flakes, if using.

Open the tomato cans and pour their contents directly into the pot one at a time (no need to crush the tomatoes; they'll be passed through the food mill). Fill one empty tomato can with 1 cup [240 ml] of cold water, swirl, and dump that tomato water into the second can, swirl, and dump it out into the third can, and add the tomato water to the pot plus 6 cups [1.5 L] of water. You will have a watery, tomato brothy—looking pot of love in front of you. Raise the heat to high until it begins to boil, then lower the heat to a simmer.

Once the gravy is simmering, add the tomato paste grand-mom style: by opening both the top and the bottom of the can and pushing the top lid down to scrape through and capture the clingy paste along the sides of the can so that none will be wasted. Carefully catch both metal lids at the bottom so that you don't cut yourself (and they don't fall into the gravy). Cover the pot with the lid slightly ajar and simmer, stirring occasionally with a wooden spoon, for about 30 minutes.

Remove the pot from the heat and let it cool slightly, about 20 minutes. Meanwhile, fit a food mill with the smallest disk and place it over a large, shallow bowl. Using an 8 oz [240 ml] ladle, begin to transfer the cooled tomato gravy into the food mill and crank in batches of 8 oz [240 ml] at a time. As it passes through the food mill, it will begin to look even waterier as the tomato pulp, onions, and garlic are churned and puréed together. Be sure to scrape the bottom of the food mill so that every bit of tomato and herbs makes it way back into the pot. Set aside.

Using tongs or a slotted spoon, carefully lower the pig's foot, the meatballs, and the remaining meats back into the now-empty pot along with the juices that collected on the platters while the meats were resting. Transfer the milled tomato to the pot, covering the meats. Cover the pot with the lid slightly ajar and let the Sunday gravy simmer and reduce for a minimum of 4 hours, stirring gently every so often. The specifics of this stirring are very important, so read "Stirring the Gravy" (page 214).

Stirring the Gravy

When you're stirring your gravy, every 10 to 15 minutes or so, making sure the meat is not sticking, you will notice a ring forming around the top of the pot. That is the gravy reducing as the water steams and evaporates. Watch as the level of the gravy in the pot lowers—this is the concentration of flavors happening before your eyes! Take a rubber spatula, scrape that ring up, and put it right back into the gravy. That will help the gravy thicken. You do not want watery gravy—watery gravy is sacrilege! Or, you can scrape it and put it on a piece of bread to eat while you are cooking. (There is, however, also a magic time specifically called Bread 'n' Gravy. It happens while the pasta water is coming to a boil—or someone is coming late to dinner—and you are dying to eat. That's the time to take a piece of bread, stick it in the gravy, e *voila*! Bread 'n' Gravy.) But I do not want to see you putting that pot in the sink to wash with a thick ring around it! (My first job, a long time ago, was as a dishwasher. And it was then that I came to really understand the potential of food that is stuck to a pan.) From a cook's perspective, I would rather pass off a clean pan to the dishwasher— but if the dishwasher is gonna get a dirty pan, I'm gonna give them a dirty pan with a piece of bread.

South Philly Gravy versus Sauce and Ragù

A passionate word about Sunday gravy, the South Philly way. "Gravy" refers to a rich, meat-filled *sugo di carne*, which roughly translates from the Italian as "meat gravy." South Philly Italian immigrants from southern regions such as Abruzzo, Naples, and Calabria used this translation and passed it on to the next generation, so it took on its own regional identity among Italian-Americans in my neighborhood. In your neighborhood, you may have come to adopt the term *Sunday meat sauce* to describe that otherworldly pot of tomato and meat bubbling on the stove. But I just can't get behind the word *sauce* to describe this dish (not as a chef or a native of South Philly!). A *salsa* in Italian translates to a fast-cooked red (marinara) or white (béchamel) sauce whose purpose is as a condiment to dress your pasta. That's not what we are doing here. We're talking slow-cooking, euphoria-inducing gravy. Gravy is not a condiment; it is a meal. For more on this, see "How to Serve the Gravy like My Mom" (page 217). Or you may have come to know another extraordinary one-pot, big love dream for your pasta and called it *ragù*. What sets a ragù apart from a gravy is that a ragù includes a combination of milk (or sometimes cream) and broth. And it always includes a fine dice of carrots, celery, and onions. The meat that goes into a ragù is typically ground and often there's very little to no tomato added. My Campanaro Family Lasagna (page 132) uses a ragù similar to the style of ragù Bolognese.

One tiny little thing to add: When I refer to gravy in this chapter, I am talking about the entire pot of meat bubbling in the tomato base. Once the meat is removed from the pot and eaten, the tomato base left in the pot with bits of meat is still gravy! Even though this richly flavored gravy can be used to dress the Monday Baked Ziti (page 230), I refuse to call it a sauce.

⁂ HOW TO ⁂
SERVE THE GRAVY
LIKE MY MOM

Plate and serve the homemades
(or a boxed pasta like fettuccine or perciatelli).

Just as everyone is finishing their homemades, get
up from the table, go into the kitchen, and remove
the meatballs and meat from the Sunday gravy
and transfer to a large, beautiful serving platter.

Discard the toothpicks from the braciole so no one
accidentally eats it or pokes their tongue. Set the platter
in the center of the table with a large serving fork and
spoon and listen to the happy noise from your crowd.

"Wow! Ohhh! Mmmmm!"

Quickly run back to the kitchen and get the large
bowl of salad (pronounced "salit" in my house).
Set that on the table with salad tongs.

Talk, eat, listen, fight, kiss somebody. Repeat
until you've had your fill and it's time to clean up.

Rosie Bova holding my newborn
mother, Patricia, on 6th Street
between Fitzwater and Catharine.

"HOMEMADES"

As the youngest kid in my family, I would often be sent next door to my grandmother Rosie Bova to help her make the homemades (really, she was just babysitting me). "Homemades" is slang for homemade pasta. Specifically, the shape of homemades most closely resembles tagliatelle, from the Italian verb *tagliare*, "to cut." My grandmother and I would mix, roll, and cut the homemades on a pasta maker. Then she would leave them to dry by draping the fresh homemades over a broomstick held up between two chairs in the dining room. They would be served with her Sunday gravy and finished with freshly grated pecorino cheese. When I was a small boy, we would head over hand in hand to Di Bruno Bros. on Ninth Street, and I would delight in watching them freshly grate the hard cheese on an old cheese grater. Emilio ("Mimi") would give it to us in a plastic bag with a tie on it. And my grandmother would inevitably haggle for the price (while I'd be stealing olives from a barrel near the counter). I remember feeling very special to be singled out to help her. I know now that it was probably one way for my parents to get me out from underfoot on a busy Sunday, but the whole process of making something from scratch left an indelible mark on my spirit; a sense of confidence and pride emerged from within, which meant a lot more than someone telling me that I did a good job. Excuse me while I wipe my eyes.

MAKES ENOUGH FOR 6 FIRST-COURSE SERVINGS

3 cups [420 g] all-purpose flour

1 Tbsp kosher salt

12 egg yolks (reserve the whites for an egg wash, omelet, or meringue)

Fine sea salt

Sunday Gravy (page 211), just enough

½ cup [30 g] finely grated pecorino cheese

Space two tall dining room or kitchen chairs with their backs facing each other about 3 ft [91 cm] apart. Lay a broomstick across the tops of the chairs. Drape several clean kitchen towels over the broomstick to completely cover it. Alternatively, you can prepare a baking sheet by dusting it with semolina flour and set it aside for your pasta to dry.

In the work bowl of a stand mixer fitted with the dough hook attachment, add the flour, kosher salt, and egg yolks and mix on low speed so the flour doesn't fly in your face, about 20 seconds. Increase the speed to medium and mix until incorporated and you see the mixture come together into a dough ball that wraps around the hook, about 1 minute. Increase the speed to high and continue mixing the dough, an additional 30 seconds. Pause your mixing. The dough may have a bit of crumbly texture, so put your hands in there and give it few squeezes, pulling any sticky dough off the dough hook to incorporate it. Return to mixing, at high speed, about 1 minute. Now here's a fun trick to pull it all together: At the 1-minute mark, add 1 Tbsp of water to the dough and continue mixing, watching it all come together into a very fine-looking dough ball, about 30 seconds.

cont.

Make-Ahead "Homemades"

To freeze fresh homemades: Make the homemades as directed and allow them to dry for 30 minutes. Once dry, space them apart in little nests on a parchment paper–lined baking sheet. Cover the baking sheet with plastic wrap and place in your freezer for 3 hours. Once they are frozen, transfer the hardened nests of homemades to a couple of freezer bags, wrap the bags in aluminum foil, write the date on it with Sharpie, and return the bags to the freezer where they can stay for up to 2 months.

To Cook Frozen Homemades

Carefully drop the frozen nests in boiling water, one at a time. Give them a gentle stir so that they unfurl. Frozen homemades cook and float to the top when done in approximately double the cooking time as fresh homemades.

Transfer the dough to a lightly floured work surface and, using your fingertips, flatten the dough out into a slightly uniform oblong shape before you begin kneading. To knead, use a pull, push, and turn motion. Begin by pulling the top half of the dough toward you, then use the heel of your hands to push the dough away, repeating this motion, turning the dough each time you do so, about 1 minute. You'll achieve a golden-yellow dough ball with a very firm texture. Wrap the dough in plastic wrap and refrigerate for 20 minutes.

Meanwhile, attach your pasta maker to your kitchen counter or work surface and set the knob so the rollers are at their widest setting. Divide the rested dough into quarters. Working with one quarter at a time, pass the dough through the setting three times, folding the dough in half with each pass. Once you hear a pop in your dough, that means you're doing it right!

It is important to keep the dough well floured as you pass it through the pasta rollers, adjusting the roller and working your way from the widest setting to the narrowest setting, passing the dough through twice on each setting. The dough will elongate and become a silky and thin—but not transparent—sheet of pasta. Cut the elongated pasta sheet into thirds.

To cut grandmother-style homemades, set your pasta maker's crank on the tagliatelle or fettuccine setting (or if you have an attachment, use that) and pass each piece of dough through once, carefully grabbing your homemades as they come out the other side. Drape them over the broomstick, spacing them out so they don't overlap until ready to cook. Or place them on the prepared baking sheet, wrapping them in your hand so that they fall into a little nest. Repeat the process with the rest of the dough.

Bring a large pot of generously salted water (using fine sea salt) to a boil.

Meanwhile, in a large shallow serving bowl, ladle a generous scoop of warm gravy and set it aside. Once the water comes to a boil, add the homemades to the pot and watch them float to the top in about 1½ minutes. Use tongs to remove them and immediately transfer them to the serving bowl (carrying a bit of the pasta water with you—that's OK!). Gently swirl and mingle the homemades in the bowl with the gravy so that they are covered. Add more gravy if you like more gravy. Transfer the homemades to individual serving plates and top with freshly grated pecorino. (Or, plan B: Transfer the homemades to a large serving bowl and set it on the table, family style, but that's when you run into the "tricky noodle"—when guests try to help themselves and it makes a mess. The "tricky noodle" applies to any long pasta, so I always go with plan A.)

GRAVY MEATBALL SLIDER BUNS

MAKES 1 DOZEN
BUNS OR
BREADSTICKS

1 whole garlic head

1 Tbsp olive oil

1 Tbsp molasses

1⅛ tsp active dry yeast

2¼ cups [315 g] all-purpose flour

1 tsp kosher salt

¼ cup [15 g] freshly grated pecorino cheese

1 tsp Maldon sea salt

You just can't come into Little Owl without having one of my Gravy Meatball Sliders. In our more than 13 years, we have made more than half a million meatballs at Little Owl (I've done the math!), satisfying neighbors and friends from around the world. I didn't set out to start a meatball slider craze in New York City; I just truly wanted my grand-mom's food close to me. And they are really so easy to make because the recipe is basically a simple pizza dough recipe that includes soft, roasted garlic in the dough. Besides being a perfect home for meatballs, they can also be filled with your favorite meat and cheese combo for mini sandwiches or just toast them and top with a pat of butter, as some of my staff like to do. Or bake them off into thin Sesame Seed Breadsticks (page 229). Your house will smell so good, too! They hold in an airtight container for up to 2 days in the pantry.

Preheat the oven to 350°F [180°C].

Line a baking sheet with parchment paper and set aside. Brush the inside of a medium mixing bowl with olive oil and set aside.

Wrap the garlic in aluminum foil and place it in the oven, directly on the oven rack, and roast until very soft, about 45 minutes. Set aside to cool.

Meanwhile, in the bowl of a stand mixer fitted with the dough hook, combine 1 cup [240 ml] of warm water, the olive oil, molasses, and yeast. Mix on low speed to incorporate. Slowly add the flour and kosher salt and mix at low speed first, so that the flour doesn't fly everywhere, then increase to medium speed, mixing until it comes together as a sticky dough mixture, stopping to scrape down the sides as needed, about 2 minutes.

Transfer the dough ball to the prepared bowl and double wrap it all around like a tight package (so tight that you can bounce a quarter off the top) and set in a warm place or at room temperature until the dough is doubled in size and becomes soft and elastic, about 1 hour.

On a clean work surface, squeeze the whole bulb of garlic to release the soft interior and, using a butter knife, gently chop it until it resembles a purée. Set aside.

cont.

LITTLE OWL GRAVY MEATBALL SLIDERS

MAKES 36 MEATBALLS

Craving just the meatballs to make Little Owl Meatball Sliders at home? Eliminate the accompanying gravy meats and simply follow the Sunday Gravy recipe (page 211) exactly as written, browning only the meatballs. The secret to my gravy meatballs at Little Owl is the addition of fennel seed to the gravy pot. Because of the fennel seed, one meatball takes on the flavor profile of an entire pot of Sunday gravy. When you return the meatballs to the pot and cover them with the milled tomato, let them simmer for a minimum of 1 hour. But the longer you allow the flavors to marry and the gravy to concentrate, the better your gravy meatballs will be.

Lightly flour the work surface, turn the dough out, and pat it down a bit with your hands. Introduce the soft garlic by spreading it on top of the dough and using your hands to knead it into the dough until it is fully incorporated and you can see the garlic studded throughout, about 30 seconds. Once you are confident that they are fully combined, pinch off pieces of dough in 1 oz [30 g] portions. Using the palm of your hand, roll them around on the work surface, adding more flour if necessary, and form into soft balls.

Place the dough balls on the sheet pan, approximately 2 in [5 cm] apart. Cover tightly with plastic wrap and allow them to rise again for 20 minutes.

Preheat the oven to 400°F [200°C].

Sprinkle the tops of the dough buns with cold water, a tiny pinch of pecorino, and a few flakes of sea salt and bake until golden brown, 10 to 12 minutes. Remove from the oven and allow to cool. Once cool, split each bun in half (and fill with a warm meatball!).

Meatball Slider Party Tips

I always say that three meatball sliders make a meal, but a whole bunch of them make a party. So, if you are thinking of assembling these sliders for a crowd, make the meatballs and buns up to 2 days ahead of time. In a large pot, reheat the meatballs in the tomato gravy over low heat until warmed through, about 20 minutes. To warm the buns, split each bun in half and gently toast the bottom halves on a large baking sheet in a 300°F [150°C] oven, about 5 minutes. Remove the bun halves and set a hot meatball on top of it. Sprinkle each meatball with a tiny pinch of freshly grated pecorino (it will melt from the heat) and top with the other bun half. I recommend using a 5½ in [14 cm] skewer and sticking it through the meatball and bun to keep it from sliding all over the place. You can also use some fresh arugula leaves on the bottom of a serving platter for color and to make a base to keep the buns from slippin' 'n' slidin'. Super Bowl Sunday, anyone?

SESAME SEED BREADSTICKS

MAKES 18
BREADSTICKS

1 Tbsp olive oil

1 Tbsp molasses

1⅛ tsp active dry yeast

2¼ cups [315 g] all-
purpose flour

1 tsp kosher salt

1 egg white, beaten

¼ cup [35 g] toasted
sesame seeds

The place to be for bread on Sundays in South Philly was Sarcone's Bakery on South Ninth Street—a fifth-generation Italian bakery that is still as great today as when I was a kid. Our family's Sunday supper table wasn't complete without their sesame seed bread that my grandmother would pick up and tote home in a paper bag. If I was with her, that bread never made it home intact—it was just too good to resist eating off the heel (or more) before we'd reach the door. My mother would have some things to say about it that I can't repeat. The slider bun recipe (page 225) makes terrific Sarcone's Bakery–inspired breadsticks, just eliminate the garlic and the second rise.

Prepare a large baking sheet by lining it with parchment paper. Brush the inside of a medium mixing bowl with olive oil and set aside.

In the bowl of a stand mixer fitted with the dough hook, combine 1 cup [240 ml] of warm water, the olive oil, molasses, and yeast. Mix on low speed to incorporate. Slowly add the flour and salt and mix at low speed first, so that the flour doesn't fly everywhere, then increase to medium speed, mixing until it comes together as a sticky dough mixture, 2 minutes. Transfer the dough ball to the prepared bowl and double wrap it all around like a tight package (so tight that you can bounce a quarter off the top) and set in a warm place or at room temperature until the dough is doubled in size and becomes soft and elastic, about 1 hour.

Midway through the 1 hour rise, preheat the oven to 400°F [200°C]. Lightly flour a work surface and turn the dough out. Using a rolling pin, roll it out to a ¼ in [6 mm] thick rectangle or oblong shape roughly 9 in by 13 in [23 cm by 33 cm] in size. The beauty of an oblong shape is that the sticks on the end are shorter than the ones in the middle—a little something for every-one. Transfer to the prepared baking sheet and use a pizza cutter to cut the dough into about 18 breadsticks that are about the width of your pointer finger (just eyeball the width as best you can so that they bake evenly). Be sure to separate the sticks a bit so that they don't stick together when they expand in the oven.

Use a pastry brush or a flat rubber spatula to lightly brush the tops of the breadsticks with the egg wash and sprinkle the sesame seeds over them to coat them completely.

Bake until golden brown and crispy, 15 minutes. Transfer to a wire rack to cool completely before serving.

1 lb [455 g]
store-bought ziti

Olive oil, for drizzling

6 cups [1.4 L] leftover
Sunday Gravy (page 211)

8 oz [230 g] fresh whole-
milk ricotta cheese

Kosher salt

Freshly ground black pepper

1 Tbsp finely chopped
fresh basil leaves

1 Tbsp finely chopped
fresh Italian parsley

1 small pinch red
pepper flakes

¼ cup [15 g] freshly grated
pecorino cheese, for garnish

MONDAY BAKED ZITI

When everyone devoured all the meat and my mother would be left with some of the gravy, she would make a luscious baked ziti for Monday to stretch the gravy into another meal. My mom used ziti for this dish, but really any tubular pasta will do. If you prefer conchiglie or rigatoni, go for it. The trick to making a perfect baked macaroni dish is using a shape that can trap the gravy inside each piece so that each bite includes some of the gravy and herby cheese, as well as making sure that the ricotta and gravy mixture is very wet. Adding enough gravy and making sure to add 1 cup [240 ml] of water when assembling is key. You'll need 6 cups [1.4 L] of leftover gravy to assemble this dish. If you have a little less gravy leftover, cook a little less pasta. Also, if you have a little sausage or meat left over from the gravy pot (I don't know who devoured what at your house), don't be afraid to cut it up and toss it into the mix, too!

Preheat the oven to 350°F [180°C]. Drizzle an 8 in [20 cm] square baking dish with olive oil and set aside.

Bring a large pot of generously salted water to a boil. Cook the pasta according to the directions on the box. Use a colander to drain the pasta and transfer it to a large bowl.

Add a drizzle of olive oil, the leftover gravy, and 1 cup water. Use a wooden spoon to gently mix until well combined. Add the ricotta, a generous pinch of kosher salt, several cracks of black pepper, the basil, parsley, and red pepper flakes, and mix until the ricotta is creamy and incorporated. Transfer to the prepared baking dish and scatter the pecorino over the top. Bake, uncovered, until you see the cheese start to ooze and bubble, about 15 minutes.

Resist the irresistible temptation to taste this as soon as it comes out of the oven. If you do, you're gonna burn your face off. There will be a diabolical need, but I beg you to find a middle ground. Let it rest and set for at least 30 minutes.

SAUTÉED ESCAROLE

This bitter green in the endive family has a starring role in my Italian Wedding Soup (page 67), but it also belongs on any Sunday supper table. The rich meat on your plate will beg for a counterpoint of a cleansing green vegetable. Escarole with just a hint of red pepper flakes always found its way onto my plate next to a sausage link. The most important step in working with escarole is that you clean it really well and dry it really well. See "How to Give Your 'Schka-Role' a Bath" (page 67). Also, choose a pan that has lots of surface area.

In a large skillet over high heat, warm the olive oil and add the garlic, cooking until the oil around the garlic starts to bubble and some (but not all) of the garlic pieces are lightly toasted and brown, about 1½ minutes. Add the red pepper flakes and escarole, and give it one stir, so that the garlic is no longer on the bottom of the skillet but incorporated into the escarole. Now, step away from the pan. Don't move it; don't toss it. Let it sizzle and pop while it cooks, releases its water, and wilts, about 3 minutes. Remove from the heat and season with a generous pinch of salt. Give it one more toss with a wooden spoon. Transfer to a serving platter and serve immediately.

SERVES 6

¼ cup [60 ml] olive oil

3 garlic cloves, thinly sliced

½ tsp red pepper flakes

2 bunches escarole (each about 6 oz [170 g]), bathed, tough outer leaves and roots removed, and coarsely chopped (see "How to Give Your 'Schka-Role' a Bath," page 67)

Kosher salt

8 oz [230 g] mortadella
(without pistachios and
rind removed), cut into
1 in [2.5 cm] cubes

½ cup [30 g] grated aged
pecorino cheese

¼ cup [60 ml] extra-virgin
olive oil, plus more
for drizzling

12 pickled cherry peppers,
stemmed and seeded

2 Tbsp finely chopped
fresh Italian parsley leaves

MORTADELLA-STUFFED CHERRY PEPPERS

Growing up, three kinds of Italian peppers were celebrated: the things soaking in vinegar behind the cheesesteak stand (banana peppers); red, long peppers that would go into a sausage and peppers sandwich (Italian Long Hots); and the ones we'd stuff with mortadella mousse (cherry peppers). Growing up, a mousse in South Philly was a character on *Rocky and Bullwinkle* and it was also the nickname of my father's best friend, Georgie Sparta, a.k.a. "the Moose." Now I know better. These creamy mousse-filled cherry peppers always made their way onto my family's table for a special-occasion Sunday supper. You can find sweet or hot cherry peppers pickled and sold by weight in most supermarket and specialty delis, or look for 32 fl oz [946 ml] jars, as they contain at least 15 cherry peppers.

In the bowl of a food processor, combine the mortadella, pecorino, olive oil, and 2 Tbsp of water. Blend, occasionally using a spatula to scrape down the sides, until the mixture begins to look like a smooth purée, 1 to 2 minutes. Use a butter knife to transfer a bit of the mortadella mixture, filling each cherry pepper up like you are spackling a little hole on a wall. Place each cherry pepper on a small serving platter. Cover with plastic wrap and chill in the refrigerator for 1 hour.

Just before serving, use a sharp knife to cut each cherry pepper in half, then sprinkle with fresh parsley and drizzle with more extra-virgin olive oil.

OLD-SCHOOL "SALIT"

SERVES 6

½ cup [120 ml] extra-virgin olive oil

3 Tbsp distilled white vinegar

2 Tbsp dried oregano

Kosher salt

Freshly ground black pepper

1 large head iceberg lettuce, outer leaves discarded, broken into small chunks

½ white onion, thinly sliced into rings

Several stalks celery, cut from the heart of the bunch (see headnote), thinly sliced, plus the leaves

1 cup [100 g] jarred or canned pimento-stuffed green olives, drained and thinly sliced

1 cucumber, peeled, ends trimmed, halved lengthwise, seeded, and sliced into ¼ in [6 mm] thick half-moons

Grandmothers in housecoats and slippers (like mine) would make this salad and set it down on Sunday supper tables all across row houses in South Philly. Also known as a house salad in red-checkered-tablecloth Italian-American joints, it's an assemblage that shouldn't be over-thunk (that's a word). You should just scoop this humble, simple salad from a big bowl onto your dirty plate so that it can mingle with the still-warm gravy left there from your pasta and meat course. The smell of the oregano (fresh in the summer, dried in the winter) in the salad dressing transports me to my mom's Sunday supper table in a heartbeat. When my mom would prepare this salad, I always thought she was angry because she would smash the iceberg lettuce on the counter, stem down, to release the core; it used to scare me as a kid, but it's a technique that works! While iceberg lettuce does not have any of the health benefits of darker, leafier greens, this salad holds a place in my heart for its old-school nostalgia and simplicity. I use sherry vinegar in all of my salad dressings, but my grandmother used distilled white vinegar, which gives it an extra acidic punch. I like to use the celery hearts for this salad, since it's on those stalks that you'll find the tender yellow leaves, which you should also use. Save the outer celery stalks for soups and stocks.

In a medium bowl, whisk together the olive oil, vinegar, oregano, a generous pinch of salt and pepper to taste and set aside. Or don't. (See "Secret Salad Dressing Club," below.)

Put the lettuce in a large serving bowl, add the onion, celery and celery leaves, olives, and cucumber and drizzle the dressing all over it. Use salad tongs to toss the salad and serve immediately, right out of the bowl and onto a dirty plate. (P.S. The only time we ate it out of an individual salad bowl was when my sister brought a boy home and my mom wanted to impress him.)

Secret Salad Dressing Club

Everything about being a professional chef tells me that you should mix the salad dressing together first before you dress a salad. But my grandmother and mom always poured olive oil directly onto the salad in the bowl, then the vinegar. And I don't know how they did it, but they always got perfect ratios. And then they taught my sister. And now she has the touch. I am, woefully, not a part of their secret salad dressing club. So, if any of you out there belong to this club, membership to which is apparently passed only from mothers to daughters, feel free to use your club pass to dress an old-school "salit."

9 eggs, at room temperature, separated

1 cup plus 2 Tbsp [230 g] granulated sugar

1 tsp vanilla extract

Fine sea salt

1½ cups [210 g] all-purpose flour

Rum Simple Syrup

1 cup [200 g] granulated sugar

¾ cup [180 ml] dark rum, your favorite!

Pastry Cream

2½ cups [600 ml] whole milk

⅔ cup [130 g] granulated sugar

1 tsp vanilla extract

8 egg yolks (reserve the whites for an egg wash, omelet, or meringue)

3 Tbsp cornstarch

Fine sea salt

2 Tbsp butter

Heaping ¼ cup [45 g] semisweet chocolate chips

1 cup [120 g] fresh raspberries, quartered

cont.

BIRTHDAY RUM CAKE

Growing up, for my birthday, my godmother, Aunt Peggy, would bring me a four-layer rum cake from Isgro bakery in South Philly. Layered with chocolate, vanilla, and strawberry pastry creams covered in ricotta cream, a coat of slivered almonds, and maraschino cherries, this cake also did double duty as a treat to celebrate the Feast of St. Joseph (which fell close enough to my birthday to warrant such an over-the-top kind of cake; also, Aunt Peggy really loved me). The cake part of Isgro's rum cake is a light and airy *pan di spagna* (Italian sponge cake) that's perfect for making drunk with rum. The pastry cream is a classic Italian *crema pasticerra* that can be used to fill any fantasy of desserts, such as eclairs, tarts, and *bomboloni*. My Isgro bakery–inspired home version also features a tricolored pastry cream, using raspberries (my favorite!) for bigger big love. Since this Sunday supper is a feast fit for special occasions and celebrations, I can think of no better dessert for a Sunday supper gathering than setting a birthday rum cake alight with candles. This cake is best served very cold. Make the cake a day ahead and chill overnight before building it the next day. The recipe below is courtesy of Jessica Rayfield.

Preheat the oven to 350°F [180°C]. Trace the bottom of one 8 in [20 cm] round cake pan onto a piece of parchment paper and cut out the circle. Repeat and set aside both parchment circles.

Prepare two 8 in [20 cm] cake pans by melting 2 Tbsp butter and adding a small splash to each pan, using a pastry brush to coat the bottom and the sides. Place your cut parchment round into the bottom of each pan and, using your buttered pastry brush or paper towel, butter the surface to secure to the bottom. Scoop a couple of spoons of flour into each buttered pan; tap and tilt to dust the bottom and sides, discarding the excess. Woo! Now you're ready!

To make the cake: In the bowl of your stand mixer with the whisk attachment, beat the egg yolks with ¼ cup plus 2 Tbsp [80 g] of the granulated sugar, the vanilla, and a pinch of salt on medium-high speed until pale, yellow, and thick, about 1½ minutes. Transfer to a large bowl.

cont.

Mascarpone Frosting

1 lb [455 g] mascarpone

2½ cups [600 ml] heavy whipping cream, very cold

1½ cups [180 g] confectioners' sugar

2 tsp vanilla extract

1½ cups [150 g] or more sliced, toasted almonds

8 maraschino cherries, drained (optional)

Wash and thoroughly dry the mixing bowl of your mixer. Add the egg whites and whip on medium-high speed until soft peaks form, 2½ to 3 minutes. Lower the speed and, with the mixer still on, sprinkle the remaining ¾ cup [150 g] of granulated sugar into the egg whites, and mix until fully incorporated. Increase the speed back to medium-high and whip until glossy and voluminous, about 1 minute.

Transfer 1 generous scoop of the whipped whites to the egg yolk mixture and use a rubber spatula to fold it into the batter to lighten it up. You don't have to be too careful; you're just setting it up to receive the next two batches. Continue to add the remaining whipped egg whites, in two batches, gently folding each batch into the egg yolk mixture. There is no baking soda or powder in this cake; the leavening agent is the eggs and the air created from the whipping and folding process. Set aside.

Using a fine-mesh sieve, sift ¾ cup [105 g] of the flour over the egg mixture and gently fold until fully incorporated. Repeat with the remaining ¾ cup [105 g] of flour.

Divide the batter evenly between the two prepared baking pans. Using your rubber spatula, encourage the batter to the edge of each pan and gently level to ensure an even rise. Do not tap or shake the pans, or you will lose the air you've just worked so hard to create.

Bake until the top is light golden and bounces back to the touch and a toothpick comes out clean and dry, about 40 minutes. (You'll see the cakes dome in the oven as they bake, but they will settle evenly as they cool.)

Allow the cakes to rest until they are at room temperature, then wrap each cake twice in plastic wrap and place in your refrigerator to chill overnight.

To make the rum simple syrup: In a medium saucepan over medium-high heat, combine 1 cup [240 ml] of water and the granulated sugar and bring to a gentle boil, boiling for 2 minutes. Remove from the heat and add the rum. Stir and set aside to cool completely.

Meanwhile, take out three medium bowls and set them aside.

To make the pastry cream: In a medium saucepan over medium heat, combine the milk, ⅓ cup [65 g] of the granulated sugar, and the vanilla. Whisk to incorporate and cook over medium heat (keeping your eye on it because milk can bubble up fast), just until the edges start to bubble and you see a wisp of steam, about 3½ minutes.

Meanwhile, in a large bowl, whisk together the egg yolks, the remaining ⅓ cup [65 g] of sugar, the cornstarch, and a pinch of salt until well combined. Place a folded, wet kitchen towel under the bowl to keep it from slippin' and slidin' when you whisk in the next step.

Pour half of the warm milk mixture very slowly and steadily in a skinny stream into the bowl with the egg yolk mixture, whisking constantly as you pour. You are bringing the yolks to the same temperature as the milk ("tempering" them). It's a bit of a circus routine to pour and whisk simultaneously, but you can do it!

Transfer the warm egg yolk and milk mixture back into the saucepan with the remaining half of warmed milk and return it to medium heat, whisking steadily until it begins to boil and the bubbles move from the edges to the center and pop through the surface, cooking out the starch, 1 to 2 minutes. Remove from the heat, add the butter, and whisk until it is a homogenous pastry cream.

Set a fine mesh sieve over a medium bowl and strain the cream, using a rubber spatula to press it through, removing any hint of a lump. Divide the pastry cream in 1¼ cup [300 ml] portions among the three bowls you had set out in advance and set aside.

To one bowl, add the semisweet chocolate chips and stir until they melt. To another bowl, add the fresh raspberries and gently fold them in. The third bowl is for the plain vanilla cream, so let it be.

Immediately cover each bowl with a piece of plastic wrap so that it kisses the surface and keeps a skin from forming. Allow to cool at room temperature, about 10 minutes,

before placing in your refrigerator to chill for 1 hour.

To prepare the frosting: Remove the mascarpone from your refrigerator and allow it to warm slightly. Mascarpone has a lot of moisture, and you don't want this to be too warm, but it will not incorporate well if it is very cold. There is a sweet spot here that it will find by sitting out as you prepare the rest of the ingredients and whip the cream.

In the work bowl of a stand mixer with the paddle attachment, add the cream and, using a fine-mesh sieve, sift the confectioners' sugar over it. Mix on low speed just to marry the two and then add the vanilla, increase the speed to medium-high, and whip until soft peaks form, about 2½ minutes.

Turn off the mixer, add the mascarpone, turn it back up to medium-high, and whip to blend, 30 seconds to 1 minute. You want the frosting to be fluffy and soft, and it will stiffen to butter the more you mix, so don't be shy about turning the mixer off before you think you'll need to and running a spoon through your icing to test and see that it is thick enough to spread. If you are unsure, stop mixing sooner than you need to. You can always give it a quick whisk by hand before you are ready to frost the cake. Set aside.

To assemble the cake: Unwrap your two cakes and place them on a work surface. Remove the golden-brown skin from the top of each cake by simply running your fingers across the top and peeling it back in pieces.

Using a long, sharp, serrated knife held parallel to the work surface, cut each cake in half crosswise into two layers to create four separate layer cakes. Place the first layer on a large flat plate (or cake plate) and generously brush with the rum simple syrup. Fill a pastry bag (or zip-top bag with a corner snipped off) with the mascarpone frosting and draw

cont.

a circle just around the edge of your cake layer. This will create a "dam" and keep your pastry cream from coming out the sides when you ice the exterior of your fully assembled cake.

Using a small offset spatula or spoon, scoop the chocolate pastry cream into the middle of your icing circle and then spread evenly to the inside edge of your icing dam.

Generously brush your second cake layer with more rum simple syrup and place it rum-side down onto your prepared layer, pressing lightly to secure it to your frosting and chocolate pastry cream. Generously brush the top side with more rum simple syrup, draw a frosting circle around this layer, and use an offset spatula or spoon to scoop the vanilla pastry cream into the middle of your frosting circle and spread it evenly to the inside edge of your frosting dam. Repeat the steps with a third cake layer, brushing the bottom and top with more rum simple syrup, drawing the frosting circle, and scooping and spreading the raspberry pastry cream. Place the fourth cake layer on top and brush with the last of the rum simple syrup. Place your layered cake into the fridge to chill for 20 to 30 minutes, along with any remaining mascarpone frosting.

Using the remainder of your mascarpone frosting, ice the top and sides, piping the frosting all around the cake first, and then using a large offset spatula to smooth out the piped lines. Let it look rustic and do not worry too much here!

Spread the almonds out onto a sheet pan and, holding the cake in one hand, scoop almonds into the other and press them lightly into the sides around the cake. You could even sprinkle them across the top, if you like. Be creative and make it yours!

For a classic finish, pipe small rosettes evenly around the top. Lining these up across from one another each time, you can plot out 8 rosettes, popping a maraschino cherry (if using) onto each. Ta-da! Showstopper. Add candles and celebrate!

Fulginiti and Bova families. My uncle Ritchie and my mother are on the bottom right.

CHAPTER

8

Desserts

ℒ Desserts

We don't have a pastry chef at Little Owl because it is just too small for another person in the kitchen. So, from the get-go I decided to create desserts for my restaurant that were easy to make, delicious to eat, and used excellent ingredients that didn't take up too much room on my shelves (I even use panko bread crumbs in dessert because they're always in stock!). In these desserts, you'll find where savory meets sweet in Rosie Bova's Fennel Biscotti (page 249). They are wonderful dipped in wine, and although Rosie herself wasn't much of a wine lover, I think she would approve. And you'll find a Philly Cheesecake (page 255) that is so incredibly luscious, I hope that you'll make it a favorite. And of course, the seasons drive my menu, so any number of seasonal fruits can be vamped on in my Strawberry Rhubarb Crisp (page 257). Chef Jimmy Bradley taught me so much about cooking and how to enjoy life. And that included not skimping on dessert.

Rosie Bova's Fennel Biscotti **249**

Snickerdoodles *with Salted Caramel* **250**

Vanilla Bean Panna Cotta
with Citrus and Mint **252**

Philly Cheesecake
with Blueberry Agave Sauce **255**

Strawberry Rhubarb Crisp **257**

Brandied Cherry and
Apple Strudel **259**

Mascarpone Semifreddo **261**

ROSIE BOVA'S FENNEL BISCOTTI

MAKES ABOUT
36 BISCOTTI

½ cup [100 g]
granulated sugar

½ cup [100 g] packed
brown sugar

4 Tbsp [55 g] butter,
at room temperature

3 eggs, lightly beaten

1 Tbsp fennel seed

3 cups [420 g] all-
purpose flour

1 Tbsp baking powder

Kosher salt

½ cup [60 g] chopped
almonds

Cookies are like meatballs: When the going gets rough, they make me feel better. My mom says I was born with a Stella D'oro S-shaped breakfast cookie in my mouth. My mom-mom's biscotti, fragrant from bits of fennel seed, beg you to dip them into a glass of dessert wine and nibble your cares away. And there is no better big love feeling to me than having her meatballs around or having these crunchy cookies after dinner. Keep them stored in an airtight container or an old cookie tin on your counter. You'll bake them twice, just like the name says (bet you knew that, didn't you?).

Preheat the oven to 350°F [180°C]. Line a baking sheet with parchment paper.

In a large bowl, combine the sugars and butter and beat with a wooden spoon until very creamy. Add the eggs and fennel seed and mix until well combined. Add the flour, baking powder, and a pinch of salt and stir until the mixture is uniform. Add the chopped almonds and gently stir until combined.

Turn the dough out onto a clean work surface and, using a bench scraper, divide the dough into two portions. Using your hands, shape each dough portion into a log about 10 in [25 cm] long and 1 in [2.5 cm] thick. Place the dough logs 4 in [10 cm] apart on the prepared baking sheet. Using the palm of your hand, flatten each dough log so that it is about 2 in [5 cm] wide. Bake until the ends begin to brown slightly, 20 to 25 minutes. Allow to cool completely before proceeding with the second bake.

Slice each dough log into ½ in [12 mm] thick diagonal slices and arrange them cut-side down on the same baking sheet. Bake until the bottoms brown, 8 to 10 minutes. Turn them over and bake the other side, until very crisp and nicely browned, an additional 3 to 5 minutes. Cool completely on a rack before eating (it's hard to resist, I know). Keep a pile of them on your countertop, stored in a paper bag or tin for up to 1 week. Or gift them, like my mom-mom used to do.

½ cup [100 g] sparkling,
sanding, or large crystal
sugar, for rolling (Bob's
Red Mill is best!)

1¼ cups [275 g] butter,
at room temperature

1 cup [200 g] packed
dark brown sugar

½ cup [100 g]
granulated sugar

1 Tbsp vanilla bean paste

1 egg, plus 1 egg yolk

2½ cups [350 g]
all-purpose flour

1 tsp baking soda

½ tsp cinnamon

1½ tsp cream of tartar

½ tsp kosher salt

10 oz [280 g] salted
caramels, cut into ¼ in
[6 mm] chunks (Fleur
de Sel caramels from
Trader Joe's are great,
but any soft, salted
caramel will work fine)

SNICKERDOODLES
with Salted Caramel

A member of my staff, Amy Donato, started "Cookie Wednesday" at
Market Table, my restaurant with my business partner and executive chef,
Mike Price. She began with fabulous old-school creations like chocolate
chip and oatmeal raisin. Then, week by week, she wowed us with her
distinctive concoctions like banana cream pie, Fluffernutter, and jam and
cheese. But my all-time favorite are her snickerdoodles. Their soft and
gooey caramel filling says love at first sight. "Cookie Wednesday" grew
into "Cookie Every Day" when I began to offer Donato's cookies on my
dessert menu. Since then, Amy has become an expert cookie baker, filling
special orders for guests at Little Owl, The Clam, Market Table, and Little
Owl private events!

Preheat the oven to 350°F [180°C]. Line a baking sheet with
parchment paper. Set aside. In a shallow bowl, add the sparkling
sugar and set aside.

In a small saucepan over medium-high heat, melt the butter.
Continue to cook until the butter foams and takes on an amber
hue (going from light tan to toasty brown), tiny bubbles form,
brown specks appear on the bottom of the saucepan, and a nutty
aroma is in the air, about 2 minutes. Transfer the butter to a
heat-proof bowl (use a rubber spatula to scrape the bottom and
get all the browned bits!) and let cool, about 30 minutes.

In the work bowl of a stand mixer fitted with the paddle attachment, combine the melted butter, both sugars, and the vanilla
bean paste and mix on low speed until uniform. Add the whole
egg and mix until combined, about 30 seconds, then add the egg
yolk, mixing on low speed, until all is creamy and incorporated,
about 30 seconds.

Set a fine-mesh sieve over a large mixing bowl and sift the flour,
baking soda, cinnamon, cream of tartar, and salt. Slowly add the
sifted ingredients to the mixer bowl with the wet mixture, using
a rubber spatula to scrape down the sides of the bowl with each
addition. Mix on low speed until the dough doesn't stick to the
sides, about 2 minutes (it will look a grease ball!).

Use a medium cookie scoop to drop one dough ball at a time into the palm of your hand and flatten it slightly, add one chunk of caramel, pinch the edges together to tuck it in, then gently roll it back into a smooth ball, sealing any cracks in the dough so that the caramel doesn't escape. Lightly roll the caramel-filled cookie dough ball in the bowl of sparkling sugar and place on your prepared baking sheet.

Bake until the tops crackle slightly and the edges are just lightly browned, 6 to 8 minutes. Transfer the cookies to a wire rack to cool completely before serving. Transfer to an airtight container and store on your counter for up to 1 week.

SERVES 6

4 cups [960 ml]
heavy cream

⅓ cup [65 g]
sugar

1 Tbsp bourbon
vanilla extract

1 vanilla bean

5 sheets of gelatin, or
5 tsp powdered gelatin

Citrus and Mint Salad
(recipe follows), for serving

VANILLA BEAN PANNA COTTA
with Citrus and Mint

Panna cotta ("cooked cream" in Italian) is so silky, rich, and easy to whip up (if you can make Jell-O, you can make panna cotta) that I consider it the fanciest unfancy dessert ever. And I love to get funky with it by using glass ramekins, small glass jars, Little Owl stemless wineglasses, or even small coffee mugs as vessels to serve it in. Or chill it in colossal ice cube trays and pop out little squares. This creamy vanilla treat is a blank canvas for lots of fruit toppings, but I am a sucker for sunshiny Citrus and Mint Salad (below left). Note: If you are using gelatin sheets, be careful that they don't stick together; they are very thin, and you need to pull them apart. Too much gelatin will make your panna cotta's texture too firm; it's all about the creamy jiggety-jig-jiggle!

CITRUS AND MINT SALAD

SERVES 6

1 medium orange (blood, Cara Cara, or navel), cut into supremes (see page 70)

1 large pink grapefruit, cut into supremes (see page 70)

1 Tbsp fresh lime zest

1 Tbsp finely chopped fresh mint leaves

In a small bowl, add the citrus segments, lime zest, and mint. Mix to combine and serve alongside or on top of Vanilla Bean Panna Cotta.

In a medium saucepan over medium-high heat, add the heavy cream, sugar, and vanilla extract and whisk gently to combine. Use a sharp knife to slice the vanilla bean open and use the back of the knife to scrape out the seeds. Add both bean and seeds to the mixture. Bring the cream to a boil and then lower the heat to a simmer and cook, whisking occasionally, for an additional 1 to 2 minutes.

Working with one sheet at a time, add the gelatin and whisk into the cream mixture until it completely dissolves, about 10 seconds. The cooking cream bubbles up fast, so lower the heat if needed. Continue cooking and whisking until you have used up all the gelatin sheets. When the last sheet is dissolved, remove the cream from the heat.

Set a fine-mesh sieve over a large glass pitcher and strain the cooked cream, using a rubber spatula to push it through the sieve, giving that vanilla bean on the bottom of the sieve a smash or two with your spatula so you can eke out all the flavor.

Divide the cooked cream among your favorite vessels (see headnote) in 5 oz [150 ml] portions, filling about 1 in [2.5 cm] from the top. Cool at room temperature, then cover with plastic wrap and refrigerate for a minimum of 4 hours or up to 2 days. Serve with Citrus and Mint Salad.

PHILLY CHEESECAKE
with Blueberry Agave Sauce

Growing up, my mom would say, "It's not cheesecake if it doesn't have cracks on the top." And truly, I am all for the glory of imperfection in nature and in cooking (you'll notice that my pancakes aren't perfectly round, my breadsticks aren't uniformly cut, and achieving a gorgeous burst of flavor surprise from an imperfectly torn, large piece of herb in a salad comes from not wanting to be too perfect). But, I want my cheesecake smooth, rich, luscious, and crack-free. Sorry, Mom. This recipe calls for a water bath so that the center stays moist and the edges don't brown and dry, which prevents cracks from forming. It's old-school mom-mom Philadelphia-style cheesecake meets professional chef moves. P.S. If I had to choose a last supper, it would be Spaghetti and Clams (page 107), Jonathan Waxman's roasted chicken (from his book *Italian, My Way*) and this Philadelphia-style (sorry, New York) cheesecake for dessert.

Preheat the oven to 275°F [135°C]. Use your hands to butter the bottom and sides of a 10 in [25 cm] springform pan. Wrap the outside of the pan, including the bottom, in a double layer of aluminum foil. Set aside.

In the bowl of a food processor, combine the graham crackers and cinnamon and process until very fine. Add the melted butter and pulse until it forms a fine crumb mixture. Transfer the mixture to the prepared pan and, at first, use your hands to press it down, creating a layer of crust that climbs up the sides of the pan. Once it is evenly spread, use the bottom of a measuring cup (or a juice glass) to press it down to make a firm base. Bake until deep brown and set, about 15 minutes. Let cool completely at room temperature.

Meanwhile, in the bowl of a stand mixer fitted with the paddle attachment, add the cream cheese and sour cream and beat on medium speed until smooth, about 1 minute. Add the sugar, vanilla, lemon juice, and lemon zest and continue beating until creamy and well combined, 1 to 2 minutes. Stop and use a rubber spatula to scrape down the sides of the bowl.

cont.

16 graham crackers, 3 by 5 in [7.5 by 12 cm] each

⅛ tsp cinnamon

5 Tbsp [70 g] butter, melted

Two 8 oz [230 g] packages Philadelphia brand cream cheese, at room temperature

16 oz [455 g] sour cream, at room temperature

1 cup [200 g] sugar

1 Tbsp vanilla extract

1 Tbsp fresh lemon juice

1 Tbsp lemon zest

4 eggs, at room temperature

Blueberry Agave Sauce (recipe follows), for serving

BLUEBERRY AGAVE SAUCE

MAKES ABOUT 1 CUP
[240 ML]

2 cups [180 g] fresh blueberries

1 Tbsp fresh lemon juice

1 Tbsp unrefined, organic agave nectar

2 cinnamon sticks

In a small saucepan over low heat, combine the blueberries, lemon juice, agave nectar, and cinnamon sticks. Cook until the blueberries release their juices, bubble up, and soften, 10 to 12 minutes. Set aside to cool, removing the cinnamon sticks before transferring to an airtight container to chill before serving with Philly Cheesecake.

Now, let's talk: One at a time, crack an egg right into the mixture and, on medium speed, beat until the egg is fully incorporated, about 1 minute, before continuing with the next egg, repeating cracking and incorporating until you have added all of your eggs. Or, if you are a little nervous about getting eggshell in the mix, crack them, one at a time, into a small bowl, lightly beat, and add to the mixture, still making sure each egg is incorporated before continuing with the remaining eggs. Be you.

Transfer the mixture to the prepared pan, giving the pan a tap or two on your countertop to release any air bubbles. Using an offset spatula, smooth out the top.

Fill a roasting pan 1 in [2.5 cm] deep with hot water. Place the springform pan in the roasting pan and bake until just set—it should have a little jiggle to it when you shake the pan, about 1 hour. Transfer to a wire rack to cool completely before refrigerating for a minimum of 4 hours or overnight. To serve the next day, wrap the entire cheesecake tightly in plastic wrap and store in your refrigerator for up to 2 days.

Remove from the refrigerator just before serving with generous spoons of Blueberry Agave Sauce.

STRAWBERRY RHUBARB CRISP

When it comes to cooking, I listen to the voice of Mother Nature. She dictates when it's time to showcase her spring fava beans, ramps, and rhubarb or give a shout-out to her fall and winter squashes, citrus, and Brussels sprouts. And a satisfying way to bring her voice into my dishes is to make a sublimely yummy seasonal fruit crisp topped with a cold scoop of gelato. You can riff on this recipe by swapping out rhubarb and strawberries for blueberries in summer and apples in fall. The almond flour topping gives my crisp a rich shortbread texture, making it extra scrumptious. Note: When looking for rhubarb, make sure you pick sturdy red stalks—anything wilted or floppy means it's old. In my part of the world, rhubarb is at its peak from early spring to late June. And pairing rhubarb with sweet strawberries balances its innately sour flavor.

Preheat the oven to 350°F [180°C]. Lightly butter the bottom of a 9 by 13 in [23 by 33 cm] baking dish by rubbing it with 1 Tbsp of butter.

In a large bowl, combine the almond flour, all-purpose flour, and cold butter pieces and use your fingertips to cut the butter into the flour, squeezing it, until the flour mixture resembles coarse crumbs with small chunks of butter throughout. Add ¼ cup [50 g] of the sugar and a pinch of salt. Using a wooden spoon (or your hands), stir gently to combine. Set aside in your refrigerator to chill, about 30 minutes.

Meanwhile, in a large skillet over low heat, add the remaining 2 Tbsp of butter and warm until melted. Add the rhubarb, the remaining ¼ cup [50 g] of sugar, and a pinch of salt and cook until the rhubarb releases its juices and softens, 3 to 4 minutes. Add the lemon juice and cook until the liquid thickens, about 4 minutes more. Remove from the heat and allow the rhubarb to cool.

cont.

½ cup [60 g] almond flour

½ cup [70 g] all-purpose flour

½ cup [110 g] cold butter, cut into ¼ in [6 mm] thick pieces, plus 2 Tbsp

½ cup [100 g] sugar

Kosher salt

5 stalks rhubarb, root ends trimmed and discarded, cut into ½ in [12 mm] thick pieces

2 Tbsp fresh lemon juice

4 cups [560 g], strawberries, stemmed and quartered

1 tsp cornstarch

Store-bought gelato (your favorite—I love mascarpone from Il Laboratorio del Gelato in New York), for serving

Meanwhile, in a large bowl, combine the strawberries and cornstarch and stir until the strawberries are well coated. Add the strawberries to the rhubarb mixture and use a wooden spoon to combine. Transfer the strawberry-rhubarb mixture to the prepared baking dish and use a spoon (or your hands) to evenly cover the fruit, like a loose blanket (don't tamp it down), with the chilled flour mixture. Bake until the top is golden and the fruit does a hot and bubbly peekaboo through the crust, 25 to 30 minutes. Let stand at room temperature for about 10 minutes before serving, so you don't burn your face off (and the juices can settle).

Spoon into deep bowls and serve with a scoop of your favorite gelato plopped on top. Cover tightly with plastic wrap and store in your refrigerator for up to 2 days.

BRANDIED CHERRY AND APPLE STRUDEL

Years ago, while working at Universal Grill on the back lot of Universal Studios in Los Angeles, Arnold Schwarzenegger called and special-ordered an apple strudel. At first, I thought it was a joke. It wasn't. I was so incredibly nervous to make it. Typically, I would have made this phyllo dough recipe because it's such an easy and delicious shortcut, but when Schwarzenegger calls, you have to make the real deal! (*Real* Viennese apple strudel dough, which is similar to a pizza dough, has to be rolled out to a very thin consistency; it's so tricky.) When I found out that Arnold loved it and told my boss "it was just like his mother used to make," I think I cried. When the presence of your loved one comes sailing back to you in a bite, that's big love cooking.

Note: If you have ever wanted to set cherries aflame, now's your chance! While the quickest way to set the brandy on fire is to raise the heat to high and let the flames lick at the brandy, I don't advise this at home. Instead, pull the pan away from the stove and use a long grill match to ignite the brandy, holding the pan away from you. Then return it to the heat to stir. The flames will die down in about 30 seconds—just enough time to burn off the alcohol. Alternatively, you can use kitchen tongs to ignite a match from a low flame and ignite the brandy that way, always being careful to keep a safe distance between you and the flames.

Preheat the oven to 400°F [200°C]. Line a baking sheet with parchment paper.

In a medium skillet over medium-high heat, add the cherries, brandy, cinnamon stick, and granulated sugar and allow the brandy to get hot, about 30 seconds. Do your flambé move (see headnote), allowing the flames to cook off the alcohol, about 30 seconds. Continue stirring continuously until the sugar is dissolved, the brandy reduces by more than half, and the cherries get nice and plump, about 3 minutes. Discard the cinnamon stick and set aside the brandied cherries.

cont.

SERVES 8

½ cup [70 g]
dried cherries

¼ cup [60 ml] brandy
(choose a good one
that you would also
like to drink!)

1 cinnamon stick

1 Tbsp granulated sugar,
plus more for sprinkling

3 medium apples, peeled,
cored, quartered, then
sliced crosswise into ¼ in
[6 mm] thick slices

⅔ cup [40 g] panko
bread crumbs

¼ tsp ground cinnamon

2 Tbsp brown sugar

Six 12 by 17 in [30.5 by
43 cm] store-bought
phyllo dough sheets

2 Tbsp butter, melted

Fresh whipped cream
or vanilla ice cream,
for serving

In a large bowl, add the apples, bread crumbs, ground cinnamon, and brown sugar and toss it together with your hands until well combined. Transfer the brandied cherries to the bowl, using a rubber spatula to scrape everything from the skillet. Use a wooden spoon to mix and set aside.

Place the phyllo sheets on a clean work surface and keep the stack under a clean, damp kitchen towel so they don't dry out while you work. Working with one sheet at a time, use a pastry brush to brush a sheet with a bit of melted butter. Top that sheet with another sheet of phyllo and brush with butter. Repeat the layering and buttering with each of the remaining sheets until you have used up most of the butter, reserving some to brush the outside of the rolled strudel before baking.

Spread the apple-cherry filling over the top of the phyllo sheet stack, leaving a 1 in [2.5 cm] border. Beginning with the long end, roll it closed like a jelly roll. Pinch the ends of the strudel shut and transfer, seam-side down, to the prepared baking sheet. Brush the top with a thin coating of remaining melted butter and sprinkle with granulated sugar.

Bake until the top is crispy and brown, 18 to 20 minutes. Allow to cool a bit before slicing and serving with fresh whipped cream or vanilla ice cream. Transfer any leftovers to an airtight container and store in your refrigerator for up to 2 days.

MASCARPONE SEMIFREDDO

Because space is so limited at Little Owl, our desserts are served with scoops of gelati from New York City's Il Laboratorio del Gelato—they make the most delightful array of gelati and seasonal fruit sorbets that taste homemade. But to capture that homemade ice cream feeling without the need for an ice cream maker, a semifreddo hits the spot! *Semifreddo* means "partially frozen" and the texture is a cross between an airy gelato and a mousse. Serve the raspberries alongside the semifreddo for a big love treat any day of the week. (P.S. If you haven't already figured it out by now, raspberries make me crazy. I love them, I love them. And I want them every day in everything.) Make the semifreddo at least 8 hours ahead of serving to give it ample time to set.

Line a 9 by 5 by 3 in [23 by 12 by 7.5 cm] loaf pan with a large piece of plastic wrap, leaving enough excess to hang over the sides. Set aside.

In the bowl of a stand mixer, using the whisk attachment, add the egg yolks and sugar and beat on high speed until the mixture is thick and pale, about 1 minute. Add the mascarpone, vanilla, and lemon zest and continue whisking until creamy, stopping occasionally to scrape down the sides of the bowl, 1 to 2 minutes more.

In a large bowl, using a hand mixer, beat the egg whites on high speed until they hold stiff peaks (if you lift up the whisk, the egg will keep its form), 2 to 3 minutes. Use a rubber spatula to gently transfer and fold the egg whites into the mascarpone mixture until it is uniformly incorporated.

Transfer the mixture to the prepared loaf pan, folding the excess plastic wrap over the top and then wrapping it tightly all around like a package with additional plastic wrap to seal it completely. Freeze the mixture for a minimum of 8 hours or overnight.

In a small bowl, combine the raspberries, honey, and thyme and let sit for 5 minutes.

Before serving, run the sides of the baking pan under hot water to loosen it and then flip the pan onto a serving platter. Slice the semifreddo into thick slices (just like cake!) and top with the raspberries. Serve immediately.

SERVES 8

6 eggs, at room temperature (let cold eggs sit at least 30 minutes), separated

⅔ cup [130 g] sugar

1 lb [455 g] mascarpone cheese

1 Tbsp vanilla extract

2 tsp freshly grated lemon zest

1 pint [400 g] fresh raspberries

1 Tbsp honey

1 Tbsp finely chopped fresh thyme

AFTERWORD

In August 2011, Hurricane Irene was barreling north and heading straight for the mid-Atlantic coastline. With wind predicted to blow the windows out of skyscrapers, we all prepared to batten down the hatches in the West Village. On nights like this, in neighborhoods across New York City, a whiff of an impending snowstorm, rainstorm, or otherwise dramatic weather event sends throngs of hungry, hunkered-down locals to whatever neighborhood restaurants and bars are within their walking distance. And it was for this reason—a kinship and responsibility we felt for our neighbors and regulars—that we kept Little Owl and Market Table (my restaurant with my business partner Mike Price) open for abbreviated dinner services. We also had a birthday party scheduled at Little Owl the Venue that we decided to honor.

But with a mass transit shutdown amid the threat of Irene, on this particular Saturday night, I staffed all three locales with a skeleton crew of employees who lived in Manhattan, and I took a place cooking on the line in Market Table's kitchen for my partner Mike, leaving Little Owl's kitchen in the hands of my trusted sous chef, Gustavo.

In December 2010, a snowstorm buried New York City, and the mayor's office was dealt some tough blowback from their inadequate if not ill-prepared and dangerous response that left New York City crippled. If Bloomberg wasn't taking any chances, then neither was I. And to top it all off, there were rumors of looting afoot among the small business owners in the West Village. While long the home of artists, bohemians, and eccentrics, our Greenwich Village has developed into an affluent starter neighborhood for a transient, younger crowd, as well as celebrities who can afford some of our most beautiful landmark buildings. But we were not without our share of New York City looters who were apt to go for broke during a power outage. And power outages and major flooding were expected across the five boroughs.

We pulled the plug on service around 9 p.m. and before I left for the night, I directed the manager to give me all the cash to take home for safekeeping. With Little Owl only a few short blocks from Market Table, I rolled up on my hoverboard scooter (remember those things?) to collect that night's cash from my maître d', Chris. We had a few quick pops and off I went to Little Owl's Venue, at 93 Greenwich Avenue, with $8,000 in cash stuffed in my pockets, to pick up the rest of the business's cash and provide closing instructions for my manager Jon.

I never made it there.

When I got to the corner of Bleecker and Charles, a little white car ran a red light. I slammed on the breaks of my scooter and flew across the hood of the car. The side-view mirror hit me squarely on the hip as I spun through the air and landed on my head on the asphalt. In shock, I picked myself up and headed home. One look in my bathroom mirror snapped my badly shaken self into reality and I called Chris at Little Owl to take me to Bellevue Hospital in the East Village.

I suffered a busted skull, a fractured supra-orbital, impaired vision on my left side, and a fractured C1 vertebrae. I also broke my pinky. But, I didn't know I broke my pinky until 3 months later. Because the hospital evacuated me at 4 a.m.

The next morning, the now-downgraded Tropical Storm Irene pounded New York City with heavy rain and winds, while I drifted off under a stupor of painkillers. As soon as the Holland Tunnel reopened, my mom, Patricia, was able to come into the city from Phila-delphia to take me in for my follow-up. And of course, she cooked for me—as only your mother can. Gustavo and my staff also came to see me and nurse me back to health with some of my favorite dishes. They are my family, as much as my own back home in Philly.

Since that night, I haven't worked a complete dinner service at either of my restaurants, making it only until 10 p.m. or so. My chronic sciatica makes it impossible to withstand a full shift.

Each year, we celebrate the anniversary of Little Owl's opening. And each year, I am so grateful that Little Owl is still so well loved and thriving, especially in the cutthroat world of New York City restaurants. The feeling of big love extends beyond cooking and running a restaurant; it is a practice of kindness that we, my staff and Little Owl family, wish to cultivate and put out into the world. And that practice is needed now, more than ever. Once upon a time, I was one little white car away from losing it all.

Here's to cooking, eating, and living with boundless joy, appreciation, and care that is big love.

— **Joey Campanaro**
June 2019

ACKNOWLEDGMENTS

Chronicle Books, thank you for believing in this book and bringing big love cooking to the world. Camaren Subhiyah, my editor, you have my sincere gratitude for your tremendous support and vision. My book designer, Lizzie Vaughan, you were instrumental in bringing this book to life and an absolute pleasure to work with. And to Sarah Billingsley and Claire Gilhuly, for carrying us to the finish line!

Janis Donnaud, you are not only my agent but also my treasured neighbor for more than a decade. Thank you so much for your support. Theresa Gambacorta, you are onto something and I want to write more beautiful books with you. Thank you! Calvin Trillin, you keep the bohemian spirit of the Village alive and always give all of us at Little Owl a giggle. You're so witty and funny and I thank you for your wonderful foreword. Con Poulos, thank you for capturing the spirit of these dishes, my food, my family, the Little Owl, and this book with your stunning photographs, and Paul Grimes, thank you for making my food look as good as I know it tastes! Together you were my dream team. Thank you to my family: my sister, Michele, for your support; my brother Lou, for getting me my first job in New York City; and my brother Michael, for saving my life at the House of Industry (and being my fishing partner!). And thank you to my cousin Thomas Campanaro, for being the fourth brother on the third floor. Thank you, executive chef of The Clam, Mike Price, with whom I have worked since 1994. You're my culinary brother! Jimmy Bradley, you took a chance on me and gave me my first executive chef job in New York City. Thank you. And Jonathan Waxman, thank you for your friendship, guidance, and making me ask myself, "Do you love it?"

Thank you to my chef de cuisine "Gustavo" Miguel Angelo Machuca Pena, "I love to cook, but not like this." I love to cook with you. And my big love to the Little Owl Squad, front of the house and back of the house, for continuing to make Little Owl the most special corner in the neighborhood. Thanks to Fred Rudd and The Rudd Family for sharing your space with us. I wouldn't want my restaurant in any other building in NYC. I have tremendous gratitude for Maggie Baisch Hollingsworth and all of my business partners who make coming to work every day not just a reality but also a pleasure! And thank you to the Little Owl Events Team at Little Owl the Venue and Little Owl the Townhouse for the use of your spaces and being so great at what you do! Thank you, Robert Crosson, for being the skipper of Little Owl the Venue. Thank you, Jessica Rayfield, for your perfect rum cake, and Amy Donato, for your amazing snickerdoodle cookies. Thank you,

Amy Tucker, for living. And for diligently
testing every recipe in this book. My sincer-
est thanks to the recipe-testing support team
of Austin Cook, my best good buddy August
Goulet, and Racielle Cuervas, for always
being at the ready to help. Thank you, Eric
Tevrow and Angelo Ruvio of Early Morning
Seafood, for providing me with the best fish
available in New York City. And Pat LaFreida,
for providing me with the best meat since
2001. Special thank-you to my neighborhood
butcher, Joe Ottomanelli and his family at O.
Ottomanelli & Sons Meat Market—it's where
you go to get your meat in Greenwich Village.
A tremendous thank-you to all of my Little
Owl friends and neighbors, especially Richard Eric Weigle, the president of the Grove
Street Block Association, for your birdhouse
vision, and to our treasured customers. You
know where to eat and I love to feed you!
Thank you to the legendary Mimi Sheraton,
for generously lending me her timeless and
unique tableware to adorn Con's amazing
photos, and Julie at Fishs Eddy in Manhattan, for loaning our team props and plates.
Thank you, too, Claire Torino and David
"Bear" Boland, for your treasured platters.
And thank you to the customers who made
the fun drawings you see when you open this
book. Our favorite is the raindrops drawn
by legendary artist David Byrne.

INDEX

My mother with pop-pop
and mom-mom.

Rockin' good tunes
the food is nothing
to sneeze at!
reat music
the food
Rad

TOOLON PÖLLÖT (THE SECRET OW
SOCIETY OF TÖÖLÖ, HELSINKI)
GREETS THEIR LITTLE COUSIN
IN NYC. GREAT FOOD, NICE
ATMOSPHERE! :)

First Bellini, wow,
Fantastic!

Súpa Santa

HUHUU!

Thank you
little owl, you
are much more
than a bird to
me.

In my life
what matters
is great food,
family, wine,
and friends. The
little owl has
given me 3! ! !.

LUNCH FOR MY BIRTHDAY;
DINING WAS TRULY DIVINE;
RESERVATION -- UGH

(Haiku)

The Little Owl
is GOOD in my
Belly!!

We feel very
New Yorkish
on your great
little restaurant.
Now heading towards
Meatpacking and
bar hopping...

Anna & Adam

Little Owl
reminds us of
a cozy cottage
in the woods
It feels like home

Great
service
food &
music

Thank you

LOVE Gene EF
LA
WILL
LAST AFTER

Dear little
4 months to
girlfriend an
for a table.
it was abs
on both ac

Thanks for an amazing
start to our Sunday...
and another place to
map in the never-ending
memories of "our" restaurant

I told
draw